Tavistock
Memories

Tavistock
Memories

Recollections of a boyhood in Tavistock before,
during and after the Second World War

Trevor James

AMBERLEY

This account of my young days is respectfully dedicated to the late Trevor Saundry who was the best boyhood friend I had. We were like brothers and it was with profound sadness and regret I learned of his passing just before arranging to meet him again after more than sixty years. Rest In Peace Old Friend – You Will Never Be Forgotten.

First published 2010

Amberley Publishing
Cirencester Road, Chalford,
Stroud, Gloucestershire, GL6 8PE

www.amberley-books.com

Copyright © Trevor James, 2010

The right of Trevor James to be identified as the
Author of this work has been asserted in accordance with the
Copyrights, Designs and Patents Act 1988.

British Library Cataloguing in Publication Data.
A catalogue record for this book is available from the British Library.

ISBN 978 1 84868 740 0

Typesetting and origination by Amberley Publishing
Printed in Great Britain

Contents

List of Illustrations

Foreword

I feel this account of my young days requires some clarification about the way of life those of my generation were brought up to, a style of living gone forever (some might say for the good, others might think it sad); consequently a few salient points need to be impressed upon younger readers to enable them to appreciate how restricted our lives were, how we were taught to do as we were told without question, the discipline we were subjected to and so on. Much of this they will already be aware of but I fear many of them fail to truly comprehend the huge differences between those times and life today.

What was life really like in wartime Tavistock and after? In 1942, after three years of desperate fighting, the only effect on the town itself was the profusion of sandbags, especially in Bedford Square, where the entrances to the Pannier Market were almost obscured by banks of them and every window was criss-crossed with brown tape as a precaution against flying glass should we receive a direct attack. The same applied to the 'Council School' in Plymouth Road, and there were two brick-built air raid shelters in the playgrounds with wooden seats to which we were taken once a week for practice drill. When the air raid siren sounded, as it often did, (although Tavistock never experienced an air raid)* we abandoned our classes and went to the shelters and listened to our teacher reading a story whilst we waited for the 'all clear'. We were also made to practice wearing our gas masks which every child carried in a small cardboard box with a string shoulder sling. The younger children's masks were disguised as Mickey Mouse masks, but they all smelled of rubber and steamed up when you had them on – not to mention the difficulty in breathing properly. My most vivid memory of those times was being awakened by my mother late at night and being hastily dressed, with the wail of the air raid siren echoing over the town. It was an alarming sound which haunted me for years afterwards.

One night (it must have been some time in 1941), the air raid siren went but instead of getting dressed and making for our shelter, my father, who was on one of his only two visits during that war, told us to stay put. We congregated at my parents' bedroom window and watched the glowing red sky over Plymouth where the German bombers were dropping incendiaries. Searchlights criss-crossed overhead and the noise of gunfire was clearly heard. Suddenly there was a whistling sound overhead followed by a deep sounding 'crump'. 'That's a bomb alright', said my Dad, and he was very nearly right. In fact, it was later ascertained that a stray shell had landed in the meadows, and when I went to school the next day every entrance was under armed guard whilst the missile was examined and removed.

I recollect the 'blackout' regulations which decreed there should not be a light showing either in the streets or from the homes. My mother had some black material which hung from our windows during the hours of darkness and every gap, however small, was carefully covered up; if there was the slightest glimmer of light showing, you could depend on it that an Air Raid Warden would soon be knocking on the door asking you to 'cover up'. In the town the pavement kerbs were painted white to assist walkers in the pitch darkness at night. I remember too the iron railings being removed from the wall surrounding the parish church, and seeing workmen with acetylene torches cutting off the decorated metal railings that were mounted on the low walls in front of most houses in Parkwood Road and other parts of the town. Strangely, the ones on the wall of the Church Hall in West Street escaped that fate.

Televisions, computers, mobile phones and space travel, to name but a few topics, were undreamed of and lay in the future. A favourite saying was 'I would no sooner think of doing that than flying to the moon' in the common belief that such a thing would never happen – it was simply impossible. Today, we live in an era where seemingly nothing is impossible and much of what has been made possible is met with disapproval. My own grandmother was born at a time when there were only two means of travel – on foot or by horse and she lived to see the first moon landing. I think she was shocked and bewildered when she declared, 'It was never meant to be!'

There was no central heating in our homes – an open fire or a coal fired 'range' was what most people had and coal was rationed. Only vets, doctors and the well-off possessed cars or telephones. I recall my first ride in a car in the company of a boy called Michael Hatt, who had been evacuated from London because of the bombing and lived with a Veterinary Surgeon and his wife in Plymouth Road. The 'Vet' picked us up one day on the outskirts of Tavistock and took us back to town after which I ran all the way to our front door to tell my mother I'd had a ride in a car. Most people had no electric light. In the country there was no gas either; oil lamps were the common method of lighting after dark and paraffin-fuelled primus burners replaced the coal or wood fired stoves for cooking in the summer months. Ordinary folk bathed once, or at the most twice, a week and washed their hair at the same time; in fact 'bath night' was an inviolable and sacred undertaking. Many homes did not have a bathroom, and so a tin bath was fetched from its place, hanging on a nail outside, for bath nights when the children took turns to be scrubbed, the youngest first and eldest last. Adults bathed in turn after the others had gone to bed early. I remember several homes which had outside toilets with whitewashed stone walls and rickety wooden doors. The occupants shivered in the draught from the gaps above and at the bottom of the door and kept a sharp eye out for spiders and all kinds of 'creepy-crawlies'. It was an ordeal in winter.

Children walked to and from school in all weathers and most of us had gabardine raincoats (plastic had not yet been invented) which quickly became saturated in very bad weather. I can recall putting my raincoat on to go home at 4 o'clock and it was still sopping wet. Young boys wore short trousers and only graduated to 'longs' at thirteen or fourteen years of age; we all longed for this day, when in our eyes, we became young men. The wartime rationing meant we could not buy new clothes or shoes unless we had the required number of coupons remaining in our ration books. When the war ended the rationing continued for several years, and consequently we went everywhere in more or less the same outfits or school uniforms. All the same people generally tried their best to look 'respectable'; most men always wore a jacket and tie when they went out whilst the ladies smartened themselves up by paying particular attention to their hair and stockings and shoes; most of them also wore a coat. Casual clothing was not the fashion then so everyone 'dressed up' to go to the cinema or on trips to Plymouth. The term 'jeans' had not yet been invented, and when it was, I for one was surprised to find it referred to what we knew as 'denims' or 'dungarees'. In later life I went to sea and discovered denim trousers were worn by most seamen because they were strong and long lasting. The new hands scrubbed them on the deck day after day until the colour had paled to a faint blue, at which time we considered ourselves real sailor-men.

There were no washing machines or refrigerators in our homes. Women did their shopping on a day to day basis, at the shops their coupon books were allocated to. Nearly every woman I knew possessed a rectangular cane basket with a handle that looped over the arm. The daily shop meant they built up a personal relationship with shopkeepers and other customers alike. There was no fancy wrapping or coloured cartons in those days; everything you bought was handed over encased in paper, and larger shops sold strong brown paper carrier bags with string for handles. Tea and sugar rations were carefully weighed and put in the middle of a square of plain paper, and then expertly rolled into a cone with the paper base folded tight to contain the contents. On Wednesdays it was 'half day closing', when every shop shut at lunchtime to compensate shop workers for working all day on Saturdays. Incidentally, unlike the present day, grocery shops sold groceries only; newsagents and tobacconists sold newspapers and tobacco, and garages sold petrol and so on. Pubs sold beer and spirits and the only food you might find there (if you were lucky) would be crisps (there were only Smiths), or a pork pie at best.

Shoppers were given individual attention, interspersed with gossip and kindly enquiries about their family, especially regarding absent men-folk on active service. The downside was when your basket or bag was filled with potatoes, for example – you could depend on getting a bad one amongst the rest, something that does not happen nowadays as you fill your supermarket trolley. Supermarkets did not exist then and in relation to this I remember my father coming home during the war from an Atlantic convoy. He had visited St. Johns in Newfoundland and saw something of great interest: 'The shops over there are far bigger than ours' he told my mother. 'You pick up a basket as you go in and everything is laid out on shelves for you to take whatever you require. You pay on the way out and I think it's a damned good idea'. Prophetic words indeed!

As for wash-days (always a Monday by tradition), many of the older properties had a 'wash-house' in the backyard built of stone with a 'copper' as it was always called. As the name implies, this was a large copper basin set in a square stone or brick built surround with an aperture underneath for the fire, which had to be lit to heat the water. When hot the articles to be washed were submerged in it after the addition of washing powder, and left bubbling away for some time with a regular stir using a short thick stick, which became whiter than white in the process. Afterwards, the rinsing was done using cold water and a tin bath with handles at each end. Usually at least two or three rinses were performed and a knob of 'blue' (a square tablet about the size of an Oxo cube and blue in colour) was added to the water to give sheets, shirts, underwear etc. a bright clean white finish. It was a matter of pride and some competition to display gleaming white garments on the clothes line. The wash-house was also the place where the mangle was kept. This cast iron monstrosity has long since been consigned to museums, but in my young days, women wore themselves out turning the heavy metal hand wheel which operated two huge wooden rollers through which each washed item was fed to wring out most of the entrained water prior to pegging them on the wash line. Housewives sweated at this task in summer, and in winter endured the pain of chapped hands with the skin red and bleeding from cracks on knuckles and fingers. Spin driers and washing machines were a real Godsend when they made their appearance many years later but too late for our poor mothers and grandmothers. They were heroines in my view.

Food rationing was severe during the war years and for a long time afterwards. See the table below for weekly allowance per person:

Lard or Butter	4 oz. (113g)
Sugar	12 oz. (340g)
Tea	2 oz. (57g)
Meat	6 oz. (170g
Bacon	4 oz. (113g)
Eggs	2

Sweets and chocolate were strictly rationed and many mothers, my own included, used our sweet coupons to buy extra jam. There was no 'white' bread to be had, only the standard 'National Loaf' which was supposed to be wholemeal but was a dirty grey colour and unappetising. At least it wasn't rationed and neither were potatoes. We had only English fruit produced locally and when bananas and oranges began to appear after the war ended, many children had never seen one let alone tasted one. Devonshire cream (of all things!) was simply not available, and the first ice cream on sale in Tavistock in peacetime was greeted with delight; some of the younger children had never had any. A shop in Brook Street, owned by Mr and Mrs Dyas, shared the honours with Mr Norman Brown, whose premises were on the corner of West Street and Market Street, and I believe the ice cream they sold came from Calstock. The choice was vanilla or vanilla. My artist father made and painted 'Delicious Ice Cream' signs for Mr Brown which were displayed in his shop windows.

Did people stand by each other during those dark days as we today are often told? Yes, they certainly did. The everyday enquiries we all exchanged about family members serving overseas were genuinely made and received. In a way, it was comforting. Similarly, if anybody came into possession, by fair means or foul, of some extra rations such as tea or sugar for example, it was shared first with relatives and then with the neighbours. One afternoon, my mother was alarmed to see a straw basket bobbing up and down on the end of a length of cord outside our front window and, going out to investigate she found it was being manipulated by Mrs Dunne, who lived in the flat above ours. She and her family had come by a quantity of 'goodies' and there was some for us she was told. Just after the end of the war, when rationing was still in force, we received a parcel from South Africa from a friend of my father's. It contained tea, sugar, coffee, a pineapple (still fresh enough to enjoy) and other good things which we in turn shared with our neighbours. Surprisingly, it is now recognised how much healthier the people were who had just the basic foods to sustain them; not only that, but at 75 years of age, my wife and I still have our own teeth, most of them in perfect order and that is surely a result of the wartime restrictions.

Ordinary people did not have bank accounts and none of my family, with the possible exception of my Uncle Charlie who was self employed, ever owned a cheque book or saw the inside of a bank. It was the well-off and business people who frequented them, all of whom were smartly dressed and conversed with the staff in subdued tones – in fact, the cashiers conducted their business through glass panelled apertures with polished wood side panels to ensure privacy for each customer. To be employed in a bank was more of a privilege than an occupation, with the knowledge that your integrity was thus beyond question. Credit or Hire Purchase, as it was first called, lay years ahead and families saved up for what they wanted and paid for it when ordering. Most of us went without.

Everyone lived meagrely by today's standards, and now I am a grandparent, I cannot help listening in disbelief at times when my grandchildren are asked by their doting mothers what they would like for tea. All my boyhood I was briskly informed my tea was ready and to come straight to the table and have it. It was the same for us all and we ate everything that was put in front of us, without complaint, in the knowledge that there was nothing else. As a result, we grew up not disliking anything and clearing our plates at every sitting; to which may I add that apart from dog biscuits pet food was unknown – we were all instructed to leave some morsel for the dog or cat as the case might be.

Social behaviour has changed out of all recognition. In my young days it would have been unthinkable for men to embrace – they shook hands and that was that, whatever the circumstances. Men and women kissed only close family members when they met and most certainly not friends or acquaintances. No respectable woman would be seen smoking in the street or (horror of horrors) entering a public house alone. Even when accompanied, the public bar was out of bounds and she and her escort would head for the private bar or 'snug' as it was called. As if this was not enough to shock the modern 'Miss', the etiquette of that time also decreed that you would not take the liberty of shaking a woman's hand on meeting or being introduced, unless she offered her hand in expectation.

Men and boys gave up their seats to women on crowded buses or trains, opened doors for them, helped them in and out of chairs, and always walked on the outside of the pavement when accompanying them. We were none of us 'toffs'; it was simply what every one of us was brought up to do as a matter of course. Our 'reward' was a sweet smile and a 'thank you'. It made us feel good and the ladies felt good to be paid the courtesy and attention. May I add, most men took a pride in themselves and shaved every day; it would have been unthinkable for them to go out with even a 'seven o'clock shadow', never mind the several days growth which seems to be the fashion these days for some footballers and so-called celebrities. Men with beards were a rarity and I only remember one man in Tavistock with a beard, a Royal Navy pensioner who kept it meticulously groomed and was a very smart man in every respect. There was a saying then (an unkind one I always thought) 'don't trust a man with a beard – he's got something to hide'. 'Feminism' and the so-called 'war of the sexes' lay far in the future along with the gibberish written by a certain Miss ___ who, years later after the damage had been done, retracted much of what she had said. In the period I am writing about we were all equal and I am happy to say boy and girl relationships were entirely free of such sentiments as 'girl power' etc. There wasn't anything to prove.

Generally speaking, the behaviour of 'boyfriends' with 'girlfriends' was platonic. There were exceptions of course: there are and always were and always will be girls who are 'willing' and girls who are not, but the latter comprised the vast majority then. Sex was taboo among the young, both in practice and in knowledge. There was no sex education in schools but I well remember one of our biology teachers once mentioning the word 'vagina' to subdued gasps of disbelief from half the class; the other half did not have a clue what it meant. Not that us boys approaching puberty failed to notice the attractive changes taking place in the girls we knew, but in the main there was very little serious 'hanky panky' between girlfriends and boyfriends. Two factors which I think put restrictions on relationships were, firstly, the shame a pregnancy would bring on the family in a place where everyone was known; and secondly we had little or no knowledge of contraception. We were very naïve by the standards of today; for example I was fifteen years old before I discovered what a homosexual was and was so shocked and revolted I could not bring myself to believe such things went on.

It was a time when 'baby talk' was the norm for toddlers. Expressions like 'baa-lambs', 'bow-wows' and 'chuff-chuffs', for example, have now gone out of fashion and a good thing too in my view. Why on earth adults today have adopted childish terms such as 'tummies' and 'bye-bye', which once were reserved for infants who had difficulty pronouncing 'stomachs' or 'good-bye', is a mystery to me. Swearing was of a mild nature if it was heard at all. When I hear a TV announcer warning viewers about 'strong language', I know that what is really in store for us is a barrage of obscene and filthy epithets, reserved for the barrack room when I was young. In fact it wasn't until I went to sea that my education in cursing and swearing was provided by sailors, most of whom were wartime veterans. Yet even these rough men would never use that sort of language within the hearing of a woman. These days the very worst swearwords can be heard outside most schools and in the streets, by boys and girls alike, and I am not only appalled but feel sorry that the young have been corrupted so early in life. I can remember a young man in Tavistock being arrested in Duke Street one evening for using just that sort of language.

In those days, dustmen came up your garden path and collected your dustbin (no bin liners then), emptied it, and carried it back in. Policemen were respected and looked up to and instantly obeyed if they had cause to correct us. Every boy like me had scars, scratches, bruises, torn clothes, and muddy shoes as a result of our escapades. I once slipped leaping over a garden wall with broken glass embedded on the top, whilst fleeing from an angry owner whose property I and my pals had trespassed on, and tore open a wide gash on my leg leaving a trail of blood (it had been snowing) all the way home. We didn't even think about suing anyone – I was in the wrong and carry the scar to this day. Every train was a steam train thundering along the tracks leaving that unforgettable aroma of smoke and grease and heat in its wake. All adults were addressed as Mr or Mrs by younger boys and girls. As for drugs, never ever did I even hear of such things (and when I went to sea I only encountered it once and that was just a rumour). There was no drinking in the street and when the pubs closed, Tavistock shut down for the night – literally. It was another world.

All the above comments about life more than sixty years ago are not confined to Tavistock and most certainly not to me or my family. It was the way of life in Britain all those years ago. In the chapters that follow some readers may feel I have been over critical of my schooldays, but I have to emphasise what I have written is entirely true and reflects those times as I saw them and as they affected me personally. Tavistock Grammar School turned out some very talented pupils who did well in later life. Among them were the late James ('Jimmie') Metcalf who lived at Princetown where his father was a Prison Officer. He shared my desk for a while and returned to Tavistock in adult life to take up the post of Headmaster at Tavistock Comprehensive School. Another notable student I remember was Robert ('Bob') Pascoe from Bere Alston, a lad from an ordinary family whose father was a postman; his mother was a local Councillor and church organist. He rose to the rank of Lt. General Sir Robert Pascoe, KCB; MBE. These two examples (there are several others) do great credit to the Grammar School, and go to show how talented young men can develop outside the public school system and that chaps from ordinary backgrounds can rise to the top of their professions, given the chance to do so.

I hope the foregoing will prepare young readers for what follows. Life during the Second World War was not so very hard compared to that of the occupied countries of Europe, for example, but it was Spartan in many respects; yet there were happy times too, which in retrospect I would not have changed in any way. Tavistock has altered and grown beyond all expectations and is now home to an army of strangers, most of whom are curious about the town's historic past and that of the surrounding countryside. Perhaps this little book will fill some of the gaps with information not to be found in the record offices or libraries.

May I conclude by saying I do not hold many derogatory opinions concerning life today. Customs change with each generation and social behaviour adapts to those changes. Neither do I seek to extol the virtues, real or imagined, of the 'good old days'. To my mind these are truly the 'good days' when most of us enjoy comforts undreamed of by our forbears and the miracles of science and medicine ensure a degree of confidence that we will live longer and healthier lives. The future is in the hands of the young who are, in general, better educated, more worldly wise and perceptive than my generation ever was.

I wish them well.

An Introduction to My Family

Like most of us, I am of mixed blood. My father was George Sydney James, a Welshman and one of a family of seven. I believe they were all born in Haverfordwest in the district of Milford Haven, but the family later moved to Pontardawe in the Swansea Valley. They always spoke in Welsh among themselves, much to the annoyance of my mother who of course did not understand a word they were saying. Having said this, I never heard my father speak in Welsh and his accent was very English, not at all the 'sing-song' quality we associate with most people from that land.

Grandfather William James was a Master Tinplate Worker who, in periods of unemployment, travelled the country 'Tinkering' i.e. repairing and sharpening household tools, mainly kitchenware, knives etc. This activity kept him away from home for months and sometimes a year or more, during which time my poor grandmother had to literally scrape, borrow and steal to make ends meet. My father chopped sticks for lighting fires in a hotel after school each day and on days off scoured the coal tips for odd lumps of coal for heating and cooking at home. There were occasions when the girls 'scrumped' potatoes, turnips etc. from farmer's fields in desperation. The children went barefooted at times and my father related to me how he once tramped over the snow-covered tips in bare feet, with two sacks which he was expected to fill and carry home. He would carry one sack a few hundred yards or so and have a 'rest', walking back for the second, thus 'leap-frogging' home. When he was just fourteen he ran away to Swansea and tried to enlist in the Royal Navy but he was too young and a Petty Officer sent him home advising him to apply again when he was fifteen. This he did and this time was escorted home by the Petty Officer who needed to obtain his father's permission for him to join up. 'What's all this?' my grandfather exclaimed, 'he wants to join the Navy does he? Well, I'll sign for him to go to bloody hell!' My father's Navy Record lists his occupation on entry as 'Colliers Help' which goes a long way to explaining why he ran off so determinedly and did what he did, bearing in mind the merciless hardships and appalling conditions in the mines then. All the foregoing was not at all uncommon in those days in the Welsh valleys (or in other parts of Britain) and the coal tips were targeted by hoards of poor people seeking to eke out an existence that would not be tolerated today. Many a lad joined the Navy or the Army for a pair of boots to wear and three meals a day.

My grandfather seems to have visited everywhere at one time or another during his travels, but when my father met my mother for the first time in Tavistock he thought he could 'put one over' on the old man – but he was mistaken. 'Tavistock indeed!' was the reply when challenged and he reeled off the names of all the pubs in the town concluding with: 'seven miles from Princetown and seven bloody great hills to get there!' On the face of it he may appear to have neglected his family but in later life he found

My father George Sydney James on board ship in the Royal Navy.

full time work in the steel works and settled down. When the need arose he could always make sufficient funds available which led his offspring to suspect he had made some money on his travels and had a secret hoard somewhere. This was borne out as the old chap lay dying: 'Where's George? I want to see George' he kept saying. My father was on a train from Devonport hastening to his deathbed but arrived just minutes too late. Everyone came to the conclusion he wanted to tell him something of importance (he was the favourite of his children); maybe it was to reveal the location of his alleged money supply. After the funeral a frantic search was made for the supposed 'treasure'. They went to his place of work and even dug up the garden but nothing was ever found. It became a family legend and a talking point for years during which time the old boy was remembered with love and admiration.

Grandfather James had a brother called James (inevitably known as 'Jimmy') who had five children, two of whom were John and Mary. Mary married my Uncle Sydney Doidge, my mother's elder brother. Uncle Syd, as everyone called him, served in the Royal Navy in the First World War (and in the Second World War) and on his discharge joined a fishing trawler in Milford Haven which is where he met his wife. They later moved to Tavistock and settled there for the rest of their lives. My Aunt Mary's brother John also joined the Royal Navy and was based at Devonport from whence he often visited his sister and her family. One day he remarked 'guess who I saw in barracks last week – George James' (my father, who was cousin to them). 'Why on earth didn't you bring him up to see us?' said my aunt and so he did on his very next visit, and that is how he met my mother. Boarding the bus to go back to Plymouth my Uncle John said to my father 'you are getting on a bit George – have you ever thought about getting married?' 'Well if I had the chance to marry a girl like the one I just met (my mother) I'd seriously consider it' was the reply. And so it came to pass. As a result, my two cousins Cora and Roger Doidge were extra-special, because of the relationship between two cousins who married a brother and sister from the same family.

A watercolour seascape painted by my father.

My father was an extremely well educated man without formal qualifications of any kind. His schooling was very basic, and in those days the prospect of further education was unthinkable for youngsters from the working classes. I often wonder at the waste of potential talent there must have been and how much more prosperous and secure our country might be today had some of them had the chance to fulfil themselves. I believe his real education took place during his hours on duty on the many ships he served on. He was a Signalman, which entailed observing and interpreting signal lamp and Morse code messages as well as flag signals, reporting them to the officers and sending dictated replies as the need arose. All this was done from the highest level on the ship – the bridge where he worked closely with the officers, whose conversations during many a dreary watch he not only overheard, but often took part in. As a result my father was extremely well read, had a first-class vocabulary and could discuss anything under the sun with confidence and understanding. He was keen on and very good at drawing and painting, which not only developed into a life-long hobby but enabled him to supplement his income when he left the Royal Navy on pension in 1946 after twenty-five years service.

After leaving the Service, he obtained employment at the Signal Station at Flagstaff Steps in the dockyard at Devonport, where all messages and signals from ships at anchor in the Hamoaze and in Plymouth Sound were relayed. For a long time after the war, American vessels, mostly destroyers, were regular visitors and he got to know many officers and men quite well. Then he had the idea of painting seascapes of those ships using photographs to guide him and offering them for sale. It was a huge success. One day he had about ten pictures of one of their ships, all with different backgrounds – calm seas, sunsets, fine weather days, etc. and asked me to deliver them. Armed with a letter of introduction, I caught the bus to Plymouth and another one to the Royal Albert Gate and thence to the Steps, to await a 'liberty boat' from the ship (the only one there at that time).

What an experience that was for a thirteen-year-old boy! I was received on board with some curiosity and broad grins before being conducted to the Captain's cabin, no less. He was an elderly grey haired man of a very pleasant disposition. He asked after my father whom he obviously knew and, eying the school blazer with badge I was wearing, questioned me about my school but not before offering me some ice cream. 'Ice cream Sir? Yes please!' He pressed a button by his desk and a huge black steward appeared and took his order. I must have really tucked into it because the Captain wore a huge smile as he pressed the button again. 'Steward, Mr James' (Mister James!) 'likes your ice cream and would like some more' he said. 'Yass Suh' and in just a minute he was back with another full dish of that delicious mixture only the Americans can make to perfection.

The Captain took delivery of his painting and I could hear the ship's tannoy proclaiming 'now hear this – crew members who are expecting pictures of the ship will assemble on the after deck'. He shook hands and wished my father well before ordering the steward to conduct me to where the rest of my customers were waiting. Then it was my turn to wait until the next liberty boat was due and I joined the crew in their mess to watch Walt Disney cartoons for an hour or so. I have never forgotten that day which, apart from being an education in itself, left me with lasting affection for all Americans.

My father's retirement lasted but three short years before he died after months of suffering and pain from Hodgkin's disease, a form of cancer for which there was no cure then.

Being Devonshire born and partly raised by my maternal grandparents I have always been a 'Devon boy' at heart and am immensely proud to be so. My father's family lived far away and I rarely saw them, the result being I have little knowledge of them beyond what I have written. My Aunt Gwen married a Londoner, my Uncle Jim, who was employed as a porter at Harrow School; in fact they lived below the school itself in Harrow-on-the-Hill. Most of the family moved to the London area including my grandmother James. My Aunt Florrie remained at Port Talbot with my cousin David whom I saw only once. Aunt Gwen had two sons, Kenneth and Michael, the latter was the same age as me; then there was Leonard who was Aunt Kathleen's son, who was much older than me, and my Aunt Mabel's son Brynmore who was in the Royal Navy as a boy before the war and served throughout that conflict. He left the Navy after the war, married and went to Australia. My Aunt Louis married a Devonport based submariner and for some time before the Second World War they lived at Saltash. My Uncle Raymond was a handsome man with thick black curly hair and an easy going personality. He died in the submarine H.M.S. *Seahorse* which was mistakenly bombed by our own planes in the first months of the war. She went down with all hands. His name, R. Weston, is recorded among the others on the Royal Navy Memorial on Plymouth Hoe.

Uncle Raymond had two daughters, Joan and Ray, both older than me and my most vivid memories of them are of being teased by them mercilessly (although good naturedly). I recall visiting Gran James in Pontydawe during the Second World War when she lived in a little terraced house, exactly like the ones described in 'How Green was my Valley'. She had a small garden with clothes posts, one of which I was permitted to use as a flagpole for a 'skull and crossbones' flag I made. My two cousins took great

My father with my mother Kathleen and me aged two.

delight in hauling it down and hiding it whenever my back was turned, and of course my dear old gran unfailingly took my side and ordered it to be reinstated. On the day we left for home I hoisted my flag for the last time and pleaded with my Gran not to let the girls take it down. 'Never fear my lovely boy' said she, 'I won't let them do any such thing'. Naïve as I then was I often thought about my pirate flag still flying from my gran's clothes post.

My one other everlasting memory of Wales is of a visit to my Uncle Billy's home further up the Swansea Valley, where he was a coalminer. I recall, watching in fascination, the high overhead cables carrying huge tubs of slag from the mine to a point across the valley where the contents were emptied onto the steadily growing heaps. My uncle came home late in the day from his shift underground, in dirty clothes with just the whites of his eyes gleaming from darkened sockets in a completely blackened face beneath a battered black beret. And yes, a tin bath was fetched from its place hanging on a nail outside (just like the old days of the nineteenth century) for him to take a bath in the kitchen before greeting us. It was to be a number of years before the Unions were strong enough to negotiate for pithead showers to enable men to go to and from work with dignity. He too left Wales and took his family to live in London, but for years afterwards he was coughing and discharging black spittle. He died in hospital during an operation for a duodenal ulcer, still in his thirties.

My mother was Kathleen Mary Rose Doidge. There are numerous families of Doidges throughout West Devon, especially in the Tavistock area, and most of them are descendants of miners. There are strong reasons for supposing they originated from Germany during the reign of Queen Elizabeth I. She inherited a bankrupt kingdom, as her father Henry VIII had spent the bulk of his treasury building forts and creating the first full-time navy to defend us against the French. The Queen was desperate for money and turned her attention to the Devon and Cornwall mining industry which had been allowed to decline – especially in the Dartmoor area. In the past, the revenue from the

My grandfather Charlie Doidge with me, aged three, and Joyce Box, a playmate from next door in Brook Street.

mining was substantial, as every ingot was weighed and tested for purity upon which a stamp duty was payable to the Duke of Cornwall, a position inherited by the sovereign's eldest son. If there was no heir the revenue from the Duchy of Cornwall reverted to the crown. The 'Virgin Queen' therefore decided to revive the industry, but there was a problem: a shortage of skilled miners, which led to recruiting experienced men from abroad, including that part of the continent we now know as Germany. This, many of us believe, is how the Doidges came to Devon. I have also heard that the now defunct mine at Crowndale near Tavistock had a namesake mine somewhere in Germany.

My maternal Great Grandfather Samuel was, at one time, a copper miner living at Horndon near Mary Tavy, before he became sexton at Milton Abbot in which parish my grandfather was born, Meadwell to be exact (always pronounced within the family as 'Maidwell'). He married Fanny Titball (a name my mother was reluctant to repeat because she thought it was rude!) and they had six children, three girls (one of whom was Annie who died in infancy) and three boys. I only ever knew my grandfather and his sister (Great) Aunt Rose. His brothers were Tom, an Inspector for a railway company, and Harry, who joined the Metropolitan Police. Incidentally, my grandfather was always referred to as Charlie by everyone who knew him and that is the one and only name on his headstone; however, much to my surprise, my son discovered via the Census records his real name was John Charles.

Here was another intelligent man who never had the chance to fulfil his abilities. He was very bright at school and was selected to help teach the younger boys and girls, but necessity dictated he leave home at twelve years of age to become a farm boy for 'half a crown a week and my keep' as he used to tell me with a wry smile. When he was older he worked for the Duke of Bedford at his country estate 'Endsleigh', which is where he met my grandmother who was employed there as a cook. He later joined the staff at the manor of Kelly as a gardener/coachman for the Squire. He often told the tale of how he once escorted Lady Kelly to Tavistock by coach all dressed up in the fine uniform of that period – red jacket with shining brass buttons, white breeches, polished black boots and a top hat with a bright cockade. He had time to wander the streets of the town before the good lady would be ready for the return journey but the timing was unfortunate, as children were leaving school, and attracted by his fine attire, assumed he was a Ringmaster for a circus. They followed him everywhere until at last he made a run for it to the Tavistock Hotel in Brook Street, at the side of which was an archway leading to a brewery. There he took refuge until the coast was clear.

My grandmother's maiden name was Rogers. She was one of three daughters born to Richard Rogers and his wife Ann (*nee* Cole) of Forda Barton near Ashwater. My gran was called Dorothy Ann and her two sisters were Emmeline and Mary, who was always referred to as Aunt Molly or by other family members as Aunt May. Richard Rogers was the surviving twin (both had ginger hair) whose brother died after falling into the fire at Forda Barton. Once a prosperous farmer, he lost everything ('wine, women and song' I'm told) and ended his days as a farm labourer. Ann Cole came from Holsworthy and was a former schoolteacher. Gran always said she died of a broken heart after they lost the farm, etc. Her three daughters had to go out to work. Gran went to London at one stage and was a cook for a Bishop.

My Great Aunt Molly married Ernest Pode (always referred to as Uncle Ern). He was a prosperous shopkeeper in Launceston until he retired and went to live in Plymouth. I understand he had a drink problem and often abused his wife. She would take refuge with her parents, my grandparents, who at that time lived in College Avenue in Tavistock, but in a day or two Uncle Ern would appear to lay claim to her after which

My grandmother Mrs Dorothy Doidge (seated centre) and friends. Occasion not known.

she went willingly back to Plymouth with him. When the Second World War bombing began, they came to live with my mother at Brooklands House where, after a brief illness, Aunt Molly died. My father, who had been serving with the Royal Navy in West Africa, arrived home the same day and the first thing he saw as he came up the drive was a coffin being carried to a waiting hearse. Heaven knows what went through his mind at that moment. As for Uncle Ern, he vanished without warning when we were all out one day and died eight years later. Today, they lie buried beside my grandparents in Tavistock cemetery.

My grandmother's other sister Emmeline married a man called May and their daughter Elsie was a regular visitor to the family in Tavistock. I recall Aunt Elsie as a tall, dark, handsome lady with a lovely smile and a loving nature to match. Her son, and of course my cousin, is Colin Brash who, like his mother, takes an interest in his Devon origins and often went out of his way to visit both as a boy and in later life.

As for my grandparents, they had four children the first of whom was my Uncle Syd, previously mentioned. For most of his working life in Tavistock he was employed at Pitts Cleave Quarry (long closed and now a small industrial estate beside the Okehampton road on the outskirts of Tavistock). My uncle had a bad accident there and was nearly killed. He was what was called a 'Tapper', which entailed being lowered by a rope down the quarry face and boring holes for the explosives that blasted the rock apart. One day, the rope broke and he fell to the foot of the quarry breaking his neck and ribs among other injuries. A colleague who went to his assistance ran to the offices and got a Bible and read from it whilst waiting for help to arrive, thinking he was not going to live. Well, he did live, but only after spending many weeks in Tavistock hospital and was never again a fit man. There was no compensation either in those days.

My uncle was also the elected Trade Union Secretary, and more than sixty years later I was shown and presented with a union subscription book belonging to an uncle of my good friend, the late Mr Bernie Hext of Princetown. It contained week by week entries of subscriptions paid and acknowledged by my Uncle Syd's signatures in pencil. I gave it to his daughter, my cousin Cora. His union activities did not make him popular with his employer, the late Mr Herbert Langsford (Langsford Park, Tavistock football club's ground at Crowndale was donated by him and named after him). My uncle told me about an incident at the 'Queens Head' in West Street one Saturday night where he was enjoying a drink or two and a yarn with some of his workmates. Mr. Langsford came into the bar and cast his eye over the group upon which he told the barman to give each man a drink and charge it to him – 'all except Mr. Doidge' he added. Well, my uncle was a man of the world who had travelled and seen active service at sea in both World Wars, including surviving a torpedo attack which sunk the ship he was on. 'I couldn't have cared less about it' he told me, 'but it did hurt me when those colleagues of mine who I thought were my friends accepted his hospitality and drank the beer they were given'.

As related earlier in this narrative his wife, Aunt Mary to me, was Welsh and a first cousin to my father which made her rather special. Her smile and warm greeting of 'hello boyo' whenever we met remain one of my fondest memories. Her brother John often visited after which my aunt would keep a lookout for me and call me saying 'Uncle John's been and left you this Trevor', handing me half-a-crown (approx. 12.5p today) in addition to which there was always one for my sister Dilys. We were rich for days with that half-crown. Uncle John was a survivor from the crew of H.M.S. *Courageous*, an aircraft carrier torpedoed and sunk in the very first months of the Second World War when more than 500 of his shipmates perished. My aunt often related how he swam for his life towards a rescue boat and was about to give up through exhaustion when he thought to himself 'I'll manage one more stroke for dear old Tavistock' which was enough for him to get within reach of his rescuers.

Next in line was my Aunt Emmeline (always referred to as 'Jane'). She was a dark haired, dark eyed plump woman who I remember as always smiling and was very kind to me. My Uncle Harry Roberts was a plumber employed at Devonport dockyard for most of his life. He was a boy soldier serving in India when the First World War began and was later transferred to the front line in France where his brother Robert (Uncle 'Bob' as he was known) was killed in action. His name is recorded on Tavistock war memorial.

In 1939, when I was nearly five years old, I was staying with them in their house at Crownhill and enjoying many happy days playing with my cousin Glenda, their only daughter, who was the same age as me. One day my aunt called to me 'you have to go home on Saturday'. Well, I didn't want to leave and asked why. 'There's going to be a war' I was told, to which I asked 'what's a war Aunt Jane?' Three years later I was on my way to school in Tavistock when I made way for an army lorry executing a three point turn at the bottom of Brooklands drive, and looking up I was amazed to see my aunt sitting in the back. 'What are you doing up there?' I blurted out. 'We've been bombed out' was the reply and so it proved to have been. Plymouth was being bombed nightly and my Uncle Harry had dug what was called an Anderson Shelter in their garden, a simple underground retreat with a sheet of corrugated metal for a roof. It was a fast, cheap and relatively easy to construct refuge from flying shrapnel and debris, should a bomb explode nearby. My aunt and uncle and Glenda were very lucky not to have been killed when their house suffered a direct hit and was completely destroyed with all the contents. All they had to wear was what they had on at the time, and in my aunt's case, I believe it was just underwear and a dressing gown.

They went to live temporarily with my Uncle Syd and Aunt Mary in Brook Street, until towards the end of the war they took over the running of the 'Bedford Tap'. The 'Tap' was a public bar beneath the main entrance to the Bedford Hotel. Customers came down a flight of stone steps at the side of the hotel to gain entry and my aunt, who could see the steps from inside the lounge bar, got to know almost every customer by the boots or shoes they wore. 'Here's Bert' (or Henry or Bill as the case might be) she would say, adding 'he'll be wanting his pint of brown ale' (or whatever was his favourite tipple) and so it always happened that the man in question would be greeted by name with his drink waiting for him on the counter. They also organised and ran a darts team as most pubs did at that time. There was accommodation included and there they remained for many happy years.

My Uncle Charlie (always referred to as 'Buff' by friends and family although to me he was Uncle Charlie at all times) was the third child of my grandparents. He was made responsible for my mother (who was the youngest of the four children) when she went to school, with strict instructions to wait for him at the end of the day to be escorted home when he often carried her some of the way on his shoulder. He was a well-known and dependable painter and decorator in the town for most of his life, with a small workshop in Church Lane where he had a store for his equipment and where he mixed paint. He died of cancer in his retirement, and I have often wondered if that paint mixing in a tiny workplace with no extraction fan could have been a cause of it. He was a very kind uncle to me and in my father's absence I received from him and my Uncle Syd many encouragements and good advice. His three sons, William (always called 'Bill'), John and David are mentioned in my schooldays (Part 2).

Uncle Charlie's wife was my Aunt Edith who was one of the most cheerful and industrious ladies I have ever known and a wonderful cook. My abiding memory of her is of a happy smiling face and a welcoming greeting whenever I called. Her little kitchen was just inside the back door and you could smell the good things she was preparing before you turned the corner to get to it. It seems she was forever busy in that kitchen and I can remember trays of jam tarts, mince pies, buns and other 'goodies' just out of the oven, being generously offered and eagerly accepted (no shop goods ever compared to my dear Aunt Edith's produce). The house, No. 1 Crelake Park, was spotless at all times. My aunt was perhaps a little prim in some ways but can that ever be a bad thing? I think not. As an example my cousins Bill and John once teased the youngest (David who had not yet started school) saying: 'David, what did the coalman say?' 'Bugger it!' was the instant and completely innocent reply, to the horror of my aunt and the heated reproaches that followed.

My uncle was a highly respected tradesman and much in demand. He once did some interior decorating for a well-known Tavistock shopkeeper who expressed his complete satisfaction and settled the bill 'on the dot'. Several days later he accosted my uncle in Bedford Square. 'Charlie' he said, 'I mean no offence but the Missus don't like the new wallpaper and painting you did for us. She chose it as you know but now she doesn't like it. Can you take it all down and do it again? I'll pay you cash'. Well, of course my uncle did it for them and this time the 'Missus' herself inspected the work and gave her approval. 'Come in here Charlie' said her husband, indicating a small office, 'and I'll settle up right away'. There was a free-standing safe in the corner which when opened discharged a pile of banknotes of every denomination – it was bulging with them and bundles fell onto the floor. A number of crisp notes were counted out and that was that. The question asked is: how did they accumulate and why were they not banked with the takings?

A certain gentleman from another English county said to me some time ago he had lived in Tavistock for more than seventeen years and, as I had left the town at seventeen years of age, he was more of a 'Tavistokian' than I was. Well, my grandparents, parents, aunts, uncles and a cousin all lie in Tavistock cemetery. Moreover, I could take that man around the cemetery and not only show him the graves of so many Tavistock people I knew but could also relate where they lived, where they worked and in most cases name their children. Now I live in dear old Devon again after an absence of many years and have never been so happy or content. My deepest roots are in my home county but my heart often goes out to my long dead Welsh relatives whom I never got to know well and I regret that bitterly. When I hear a Welsh choir singing 'Land of my Fathers' something deep inside me stirs and then I know the genes are there within and my blood runs cold with the thrill of it.

This brief account of my ancestry is primarily for my children and my grandchildren, in the hope they will take pride, as I do, in the uncomplaining manner in which our forbears faced the many discriminations and hardships of long ago and that they will appreciate all the more the advantages we all enjoy today as a result of their struggles.

Tavistock Market – 900 Years of History

When King Henry I of England and France needed funds to mount a campaign in Normandy in 1105 he received what must have amounted to a handsome donation by the prosperous and wealthy Abbey at Tavistock. Henry showed his gratitude by granting the Abbey a weekly market to be held each Friday. The market has survived without a break for 900 years.

Tavistock Market Charter 1105

Henry King of England to Geoffrey de Mandeville and to all the Barons French and English of Devon and of Cornwall greeting. May you know that I have granted to Saint Mary* of Tavistock and to the monks that they may have a market at Tavistock every week on Friday. And I grant to the merchants that they may sell and buy whatever they wish and that no-one to them on this account wrong shall do. With witness William Warelwast and Alfred of Lincoln and Harding son of Alnod and Walter son of Ansgar at Stamford.

* The Abbey was dedicated to 'Our Lady' as well as the well-known St. Rumon.

The Market Charter of 1105 in medieval Latin. (Courtesy of Mr D. Cross, Yelverton)

It should be remembered that at this time the Benedictine Abbey itself was Tavistock. Apart from the Abbey buildings there were just a few humble dwellings that housed the workpeople who served the monks in various ways. All roads (rough tracks by today's standards) led to and from surrounding villages and hamlets – the main highways by-passed the town, unlike Launceston, Lydford and Okehampton which were connected by well used ancient tracks and where, incidentally, there were already established markets. The Tavistock Charter gave the monks the sole market rights within an area of 6 1/3 miles (equivalent to 2 leagues, the distance a person could comfortably walk to and from market bearing their goods) and attracted trade that previously went to the three towns mentioned. Lydford in particular was badly hit having already lost business to Okehampton market. Thus the Charter was a turning point towards further prosperity and expansion for Tavistock and Lydford's eventual decline. Naturally these changes did not go unchallenged by the local Barons. We do not know what form their protests took but in 1107 another Charter was issued by the King:

Tavistock Market Second Charter 1107

Henry King of England to William* Bishop of Exeter and to Richard son of Baldwin** and to all the Barons of Devonshire greeting. It is my will and order that the Abbot of Tavistock shall have in peace his market of Tavistock just as I granted to the church and ordered by means of my writ. And no man on account of this harm shall do. With witness Nigel of Albini at Clarendon.

* *William Warelwast who was a witness to the First Charter.*
** *Baldwin de Brionne Sheriff of Devonshire whose castle was at Okehampton.*

Market stalls were first assembled in what is now Bank Square (the area where the small car park is in Market Street) and were available to anyone who paid a toll to the Market Holder – the Abbey. As in market towns elsewhere there was a stone cross – the 'market cross' – but there is no trace of it today. The vendor's stalls were set up early on Fridays and were dismantled at the end of the day. All kinds of tradesmen congregated here selling bread, meat, fish, cheese, cloth, and poultry among other goods. Market places all over England then were known as 'shambles' on account of the filth and stink caused when meats and fish were cut up for sale and the waste was left to rot in the street. The Market Holder was duty bound to provide a system for regulating weights and measures to prevent fraud and this was usually done by setting up a court under the jurisdiction of a Steward or Reeve as they came to be called in later years (Tavistock Pannier Market still has a Reeve). His job was to collect the tolls, settle disputes, and generally supervise the proceedings. A stallholder who tried to cheat his customers or attempted to sell faulty goods could end up in the stocks. As bread was sold by weight some bakers were notorious in this respect by making very light bread – lots of air and as little flour as possible – hence the expression 'a baker's dozen' i.e. thirteen not twelve!

In 1116 the King granted to the Abbey a three-day Fair to take place 'on the Eve, Feast and Morrow of St. Rumon' (29th to 31st August). Fairs were held primarily for business and in addition to various entertainments; all kinds of trading took place from selling geese, sheep, pigs, cattle and horses to the hiring of servants and farm hands. Succeeding Monarchs granted the Abbey further Fairs so that by 1551 they were five in number, among them the Michaelmas Fair – the future 'Goose Fair' for which Tavistock is renowned. These events required fees from the vendors which further increased the affluence of the monks with the exception of three of the Fairs whose profits were given to help fund the first Grammar School in the town. With the flourishing markets and of course the existing tithes* and income from numerous properties, corn mills, and warrens, Tavistock Abbey developed into the largest and wealthiest in the south- west. It also, in common with many others, became a prime target for Dissolution after King Henry VIII assumed supreme authority over the Church of England in 1534.

Tithes: payments in kind to the Abbots or Vicars by villagers and farmers equal to one tenth of what was produced.

He dissolved the Abbey in 1539, stripped it of its treasures, and 'gifted' the remainder (for services rendered, both military and diplomatic) to Lord John Russell, 1st. Earl of Bedford, together with more than 30 manor houses and estates formerly belonging to the Abbey. The Market Holding was included. One of his descendants William Russell was created the first Duke of Bedford on 11th May 1694 during the reign of King William III, and it is to his descendants the town of Tavistock owes so much.

By 1800 Tavistock was a bustling market town in every sense with permanent shops and thoroughfares crammed with traders of all kinds whose stalls choked the streets, their carts and horses lining every available space on market days. The Friday market was one of the largest in Devon and huge quantities of meat and corn were purchased for consumption in Plymouth and other towns. A hundred years later a farmer is said to have made an illuminating and informative remark: '*every human being from ten miles around – and some from Bristol and Truro – was in the town.*'

It was Francis Russell, the 7th Duke of Bedford, who determined to establish a permanent market place and bring order to the Friday trading. White's Directory for 1850 states:

> 'The corn market is held in a building on granite arches, erected by the Duke of Bedford*
> in 1839; and it is said to be his Grace's intention to erect a commodious Market House for
> the accommodation of butchers, greengrocers, and the vendors of poultry, butter, eggs &c.,
> whose shops and stalls are now scattered and inconvenient.'

John the 6th Duke. He died that same year.

Francis implemented these ambitious plans with foresight and vigour. His father's Corn Market still stands at the junction of West Street and King Street having been converted long ago for other uses including a cinema and the present day shop. The erection of a 'commodious Market House' entailed what was probably the most momentous upheaval in the town's history. 'The Tavistock Markets Act 1859' was a necessary requirement for what was planned and after being passed by Parliament gave the Duke enormous powers. Among them he was authorised to:

Statue in Guildhall Square of Francis 7th Duke of Bedford. (Author's photo).

'construct Market Houses or Market Places ... on any part of the Site marked on the Plan'.
'stop up and abolish Saint Matthews Street and Higher Brook Street ... and open a new Street from Bedford Square to Lower Brook Street, and continue Pepper Street southwards ... into the new street'.
' purchase, either compulsorily or by Agreement, and enter upon, take, and use such of the Houses, Lands, and Hereditaments delineated on the said Plan ... as he may think necessary'.

There is mention also of a proposed Slaughter House and Cattle Market.

These measures tore the heart out of 'Old Tavistock'. The sweeping away of St. Matthews Street and Higher Brook Street left a huge swathe in the town centre for the creation of what is now the aptly named Duke Street, the wide thoroughfare from Bedford Square to the beginning of (Lower) Brook Street. Pepper Street was extended to join Duke Street as can be seen today. An even more astonishing

Tavistock Abbey Court Gate. (H. P. R. Finberg) The scene is almost the same today.

development took place when the flow of the River Tavy was altered. The few dilapidated buildings along the river bank were demolished and a retaining wall was constructed to allow for the formation of Market Road. All of which measures were paid for by the Duke.

The Market House or Pannier Market as it is now called, was completed in 1864 and was the heart of all market activity. It is a large rectangular building with an access road all around it. Three stone arches allow pedestrian access from Duke Street and another larger arch enters under the Town Hall from Bedford Square. The main entrance, for vehicles as well as pedestrians, is at the junction of Bedford Square and Court Gate and a similar large entrance is provided from Market Road. The building now became the central trading area for the town and the streets were at last cleared of stalls and smelly waste. Some idea of the diversity of goods brought to market and the tolls payable for each and every item offered for sale can be seen in the following extracts from the 1859 Market Schedules*:

For the Carcase of every Hog or Pork Pig	3d.
For Tallow of Bullocks, Sheep, and Lambs	1d.

FOR EVERY

Cartload of Fish	1s.0d.
Score of Geese or Turkeys in a Basket or Pannier	3d.
Cart of Apples, Potatoes, Turnips or Cabbages	8d.
Hand Basket, Hamper, Pannier, containing Poultry, Butter, Eggs	2d.

Bull, Ox, Cow, Steer or Heifer exposed for sale	2d.
Sheep or Lambs Skin exposed for sale	0.¼d.
100 Cabbage Plants exposed for sale	0.¼d.
Pannier of Sucking Pigs exposed for sale	2d.
Score of Sheep or Sheep and Lambs or Lambs	10d.

There were also charges for slaughtering:

FOR EVERY

Bull, Ox, Cow, Steer or Heifer	1s.0d.
Sheep	6d.
Swine	2d.

And for weighing:

For every Bullock weighed at the Beam and Scales kept in the Market	4d.
Calf weighed as aforesaid	2d.
Bag or Basket of Corn, Fruit, or vegetables	1d.
For every Ton of Goods of any Kind weighed at the Weighbridge	1s.0d.

Not forgetting 'parking' charges!

For Waggons or Four Wheeled Carriage	6d.
For Carts or Two-wheeled Carriage	3d.

Tolls required for 'exposing for sale' grains, seeds etc. included:

Imperial Bushels of Wheat	1d.
Hundredweights of Hay, Straw or Corn	0. 1/4d.
Every 56lbs. of Flour, Clover, Trefoil, Turnip, or other seeds	7d.

All spellings and Capitals as per the original Schedule.

For the benefit of young readers:
Currency. 1d. stands for one penny. 1s. stands for one shilling. 12 pennies made a shilling. Imperial Weight. lbs. stands for pounds. 112 pounds made one Hundredweight. 20 Hundredweight made a Ton.

When the large numbers of individual traders are taken into account and the fact that many of them were competing to sell the same wares, the Market generated a healthy income week on week and year on year. Fair days were a bonus.

The grand old Pannier Market continues to operate but no longer accommodates livestock. More than 170 separate stalls offer goods ranging from craft items, jewellery, books, antiques and collectables, to food and dairy products. Tavistock has had a separate Cattle Market for over 100 years; sheep and cattle are auctioned there on the first Tuesday of every month except January. Between 450 and 550 store cattle are sold

Tavistock Pannier Market today.
(Author's photo)

each month with the figure rising to between 600 and 700 on Goose Fair Day when about 100 Geese are usually sold. A monthly Poultry Sale is held each month from March to October. Both markets are flourishing enterprises and operate under the Market Charter which is now in the custody of Tavistock Town Council; they lease the Cattle Market to the auctioneers.

Tavistock is rightly proud of its 900 years as a market town. It has survived various civil unrests, a plague, and all the wars of history including our own Civil War and two World Wars. The mining booms of tin and more recently copper, have come and gone and the population has fluctuated accordingly, yet Sir Francis Drake's birthplace now is as successful commercially as it ever was. A rising populace has given birth to new shops and supermarkets, but the very heart of it all can be seen on Market Days, especially in the summer months when the streets and the Pannier Market are crammed with shoppers, many of them visitors to the town. Our illustrious old warrior would have approved.

Schools (Part 1)

Most Tavistock children graduated from infant school to the Modern Secondary School (now St. Rumons Primary School) in Dolvin Road or by selection to Tavistock Grammar School. Then there was Mount House School off Mount Tavy Road and another school for juniors, always referred to as 'Miss Balkwell's School', in the same road but situated between the row of cottages by the mini-roundabout at the junction of Dolvin Road and Vigo Bridge. Kelly College was a world apart in complete isolation in Parkwood Road on the outskirts of Tavistock. The pupils wore grey suits and black caps with elongated peaks which looked very smart. On Saturday mornings only they were permitted to come into the town in pairs for about two hours to do any necessary shopping and were impeccably behaved.

I started school in September 1939 just before my fifth birthday. Like me, the majority of working class children attended what was called simply 'The Council School' in Plymouth Road, which is now a doctor's surgery. Today it would be referred to as 'Tavistock Primary School' I expect but there were no such titles then – it was just 'Council School'. I well remember my first day, having been taken there by my mother to arrive before nine o'clock. I didn't mind going and took it in my stride but there were other youngsters who went berserk when their mothers left them and fought with Miss Davis, our first teacher, kicking and screaming in their efforts to get out of the classroom. She was an elderly woman who had also taught my mother many years before, short in stature, kindly and understanding and thoroughly nice in every way. The miscreants were gently but firmly seated in little chairs before little wooden desks and given a tiny blackboard and a piece of chalk. Soon all of us were happily doodling away with Miss Davis coming to each of us in turn to approve and make suggestions about our artistry.

Everything was basic, with wood plank floors and bare walls, and our desks arranged in rows in front of a larger desk for the teacher. Soon we graduated from drawing chalk pictures to copying letters and numbers which Miss Davis chalked up on the blackboard behind her desk. We didn't really understand what they were but nevertheless registered them in our minds to be duplicated from memory when asked. We also listened to stories and sang simple songs and nursery rhymes – 'Bobby Shafto' and 'London's Burning' were firm favourites.

A year later we moved to Miss Moon's class where we progressed to learning about money among other things. Miss Moon was a popular teacher, young and good looking with a ready smile and I think it was she who devised a make-believe shop with imitation chocolate bars etc., which we took turns to purchase from a fellow pupil acting as shopkeeper. There was imitation money as well, which enabled us to match the prices, calculate and check the change and so on. It was great fun. I think it was

Miss Moon who took us into the playground once a week for country dancing. The boys were paired off with a girl and held hands as they laughed and whirled around delightedly to recorded country music played on accordions and fiddles and issuing from an old fashioned 'wind up' gramophone. It was good exercise which we enjoyed.

We were then six years of age and playtime was a riot. Unfortunately for me it was also the setting for my first misdemeanour that earned me a taste of the headmaster's cane. We took turns throwing someone's cap into the air and catching it. My throw resulted in the cap being taken by a gust of wind and deposited in the garden belonging to the house adjacent to the school and a very upset owner crying. Miss Moon came on the scene just as our headmaster Mr John ('Johnny') Nodder entered the playground. 'Mr Nodder, I think this boy deserves the cane' she said, pointing at me. The headmaster was very well-known and highly respected in Tavistock. He was also a fair-minded man and he took the trouble to ask me what had happened, after which I was instructed to go to the front door of the house in question, apologise to the occupants and ask permission to retrieve the cap. 'Then come and see me in my office' he concluded. A very kind lady answered the door and helped me locate the cap in her garden. Then came my first audience with a headmaster seeking to punish me (I was subsequently caned for various offences by every headmaster I had during my schooldays – five in all with one exception: his reputation for 'laying it on' was sufficient to deter me from any wrongdoing in his domain). Mr Nodder's attitude was calm and measured when he ordered me to bend over and put my head in his wastepaper-basket upon which I received two firm but not painful strokes on the buttocks with a thin bamboo cane. I have since concluded the idea was to humble me and teach me a lesson. My cousin John Doidge retains a less than happy memory of Mr Nodder who often came into Assembly if there was a lot of noise and picked a row of boys at random for a visit to his office for a taste of the cane. Every boy prayed he would manage to get into a row that would not be picked on. Let me say at once, I personally never resented being caned except for one occasion when I was chastised for something I did not do, and the worst offence for which I was caned was climbing through a classroom window to get a book I had forgotten to take with me. All of which indicates the degree of 'zero tolerance' that prevailed at that time.

The next class, in order of attendance, was Miss Alford's. She was a tall lady with sharp features who stood no nonsense. She was the only teacher I can remember chastising girl pupils; as a rule, girls did not receive corporal punishment but Miss Alford possessed a long thick ruler which she used to devastating effect on the open palms of anybody caught misbehaving. My most vivid memory is of the class standing first thing every morning and reciting together our multiplication tables one at a time up to ten, during which our teacher walked up and down the aisles beating time with her ruler on our desk tops and studying our faces for signs of uncertainty or hesitation. Woe betide anyone caught in that situation for she would close in on that individual until her face was almost touching theirs and all the while shrieking out the words in time with the class. My God it was frightening, but we learned our tables and I can recite them accurately to this day or answer at once any combination of multiplying numbers you might ask, for which I shall always be grateful to Miss Alford. We often met in later life, and even when I reached manhood we recognised one another and exchanged greetings in the nicest way. Come to think of it, she was a very nice person at heart whose prime concern was for her pupils to do well.

The 'Council School' in 1944. My sister Dilys is in the front row (fifth from right). (Courtesy Mrs R. Marks)

Lessons progressed to an advanced standard when we graduated to Mrs Dunstan's class, by which time I was eight years old. Until now all our written work had been done in pencil and it came as a surprise to us to be trusted with pens and ink. The pens were coloured wooden holders with removable nibs to enable us to replace broken or 'crossed' nibs. Small porcelain ink holders were provided for each desk and rested in special holes in the top right hand corner. A monitor came round before every lesson and topped them up from a large glass container – this was necessary because overnight and in hot weather the contents would evaporate which is why some inkwells, as they were called, had hinged tops which could be closed. At first our writing in ink was often spoilt by blots (caused by too much ink in the nib), horrible streaks and splodges all over the page (caused by a nib breaking or getting crossed through applying too much pressure) and occasionally, the pen would scratch the paper and get stuck creating more chaotic ink patterns. Practice makes perfect however, and it wasn't long before we got the hang of it and produced some very creditable writing.

Mrs Dunstan was a short, slightly grey haired, lady with a son called Gerald who also attended our school. She took us a stage further than 'tens and units' in our arithmetic lessons when we were introduced to long division and multiplication. I went down with measles during this period and fell behind but she took endless trouble to coach me separately as far as was possible to enable me to catch up, which I did. My best subject came to be English. Once a week we were given large cards with gloriously coloured pictures (a different one each week) which we had five minutes to study before writing about what we saw. Sometimes we were invited to write anything we wished and I recall doing a short story about an imaginary 'Mr Funnyface' which impressed her to the extent she cross-examined me as to whether or not I had read it somewhere (which I had not) and then read it to the class – to my embarrassment (I was afterwards quite proud of my achievement). Geography was another new subject. It took the form initially of looking at photographs of famous foreign landmarks like the Pyramids, which were explained to us in a way that brought history into our curriculum as well.

By this time I became interested in reading the newspapers, particularly when they contained photos of battlefields, tanks and planes etc., all of which was exciting stuff for a young boy who did not yet appreciate the horror of warfare. Yet in another way I did. Mrs Dunstan held her own class assembly every morning which began with prayers followed by a hymn, and often my favourite one would be sung: 'Eternal Father Strong to Save'. My father was away with the Royal Navy together with two uncles and a cousin, with another cousin in the W.R.N.S. Yet another uncle was lost early in the war in a submarine. Consequently no-one sang that hymn with greater fervour than me. So my awareness of the cataclysmic events that were taking place finally dawned on me and it was no longer a game. School lasted from 9 a.m. until 4 p.m. and not a minute sooner or later. Mrs Dunstan held another brief assembly at the end of the day when another hymn was sung, always the same one – Baring Gould's immortal 'Now the Day is Over'. Then the American Army came to Tavistock – but that is described in a separate chapter.

It was sometime during this period that I was subjected to a vicious assault which I have never forgotten or forgiven. It happened like this. It was playtime and some of the older boys were taking huge mouthfuls of water from the drinking fountain in our playground and spraying it over unsuspecting younger boys (the girls had their own playground because each of them contained the outside toilets). I went to take a drink when suddenly a hand crushed my collar and neck before dragging me silently and mercilessly into the school building, along the corridor to the headmaster's office by which time I knew what was going to happen. Someone had reported what was going on. 'Johnny' Nodder had retired and his place had been taken temporarily by a younger, pale faced individual, with black hair, whom we rarely set eyes on unless he came to berate us for some offence or other, real or imagined. In my case it was imagined and without being given any opportunity to defend myself the grip on my neck tightened further as my oppressor stretched to a shallow cupboard on the wall and selected the largest of a row of canes neatly arranged inside. He then gave a practice swipe but the ceiling was too low for his liking and I was dragged into the corridor where there was a far higher reach. I held out my hand and got two mighty hits that convinced me my fingers were broken. I turned to go as I knew from experience two hits were the normal ration, but no – I had to hold out my hand for another. Then my other hand was tapped to indicate the affair was not over yet and I got three of the very best on that hand as well. All this was carried out wordlessly. It really stung; the pain and throbbing followed later, and then the discolouration and swelling were such that when we resumed lessons I was excused writing because I couldn't hold my pen or indeed the bottle of milk we were issued with in those days. My fingers were blue and as large as 'Sammy' Friend's sausages (Mr Friend was a notable purveyor of pork sausages whose shop was in West Street). Mrs Dunstan was a witness to all this from the far end of the corridor and spoke some kind words to me on my way out and I imagine she would have had one or two words to impart to the 'Head'. The real culprits laughed at me when I came back out but I was in too much pain to care.

Now there were many young lads who got similar treatment and far worse in schools and institutions all over the country, but I feel I can speak for them all when I say I used to lie awake at night for years afterwards planning what I would do to that man if we ever met again (sad to say we never did). I feel the same today nearly seventy years later. It was not only an injustice, which I could have put up with without complaint, but an unforgivable loss of self control that led to a spiteful and brutal attack. At least I didn't cry.

Then we got a 'proper' headmaster, Mr Norman Bucknell, who was a perfect gentleman, stocky in build with ginger hair and who had two young sons. He lived at Crelake Park next to my Aunt Edith's house which was number one. His was a private house on the lower side. Mr Bucknell brought a new and happier atmosphere to the school and seemed to be everywhere at once, roaming the corridors, visiting classes and seeing what was going on at playtime. Yes, he caned me too – once for hooting in class (he could hear me in his office) and on another occasion after my father, who was home for a brief few days, went to the school to enquire the reason for my late arrival at home almost every evening. I had a close friend and the two of us were fond of playing by the River Tavy after school and, more often than not, we would vie with each other in making our way along the bank from where the bridge crosses from the Meadows to Pixon Lane all the way to Abbey Weir without getting our feet wet. In part this entailed

Abbey Bridge and Weir. (Courtesy Tavistock History Society)

Mr R. Bucknell, the popular Headmaster at the 'Council School'.

clinging to the vertical stone walling with fingers and toes like Alpine climbers, all of which took a long time and resulted in arriving home to worried mothers as late as 7 p.m. when the most outrageous and woolly excuses would be made. My father came home unexpectedly and would have none of it and that led to our downfall. We were both questioned by our headmaster and encouraged to admit having lied after which we were duly chastised. My father's reaction was to the effect that if he ever again heard of me telling my mother lies another caning would be administered when I got home. That's the way it was in those days.

For all that I loved my father dearly and acquired a lot of admiration for Mr Bucknell. He was often great fun and I remember him taking a group of his boy pupils on a walk one weekend all the way to Pew Tor. We played 'Cowboys and Indians' in the good old fashioned way after being split into two groups. Mr Bucknell was one of us in every sense, banging away with two fingers extended (an imaginary six shooter) shouting 'Charge!' and even falling down 'dead' in turn with us and counting to fifty out loud (twenty five if 'wounded') before rejoining the fray. He introduced summer camps, usually of four days duration, which my cousin John went to one year at Start Point. Accommodation was an empty room at a local school with camp beds; Mr Bucknell himself did the cooking helped by three or four of his teachers; swimming, games, and other outdoor activities were arranged to the complete enjoyment of everyone.

What a man he was; down to earth yet commanding perfect respect all the time. It was he who started swimming lessons for us and I well remember my class marching up Bannawell Street to the swimming bath one afternoon every week during the summer months. We had already practised the breast stroke movements lying across wooden forms in class and it was easy to adapt the same arms and legs procedures in the water. Everyone was writhing to keep afloat with shouts of encouragement from Miss Moon and Mr Bucknell. All of us soon developed the necessary skills to swim a width, then a length, then two lengths and so on. In September we took our Proficiency Tests. It was a horribly cold morning with frost on the granite edging of the pool and we all dreaded the moment we would be required to enter the water. To our surprise, Tavistock's Police Inspector (Inspector Newman I think) was already there preparing to dive in. 'Don't worry boys' he said, 'I'll break the ice for you' and so he did, diving in as he spoke and swimming expertly up and down to our admiration and a great deal of respect. Then it was our turn.

I expected to gain a Beginners Certificate which only entailed entering the water and swimming a length of the bath. I did this with no trouble at all, whereupon Mr Bucknell suggested I go further and try for a Proficiency Certificate which meant I had to dive into the water and complete two lengths freestyle. I managed this too, although I was flagging on the final stretch. My headmaster was ecstatic. 'Can you swim on your back?' he asked me and when I told him I could his response was 'Come on then Trevor, only one length on your back with arms folded and with what you have done already you will qualify for a Star Proficiency Certificate'. I was cold and weary by now, but off I went with Mr Bucknell keeping pace with me and encouraging me every foot of the way until I finally 'touched' at the finish. How proud of me he was and of all the others who a few weeks later, were called out at Assembly to receive our certificates. As for Mr Bucknell, how could I resent the punishments he gave me, which I fully deserved anyway? He had my affection and esteem and still does.

At about this time school dinners were introduced. Two large Nissen huts had been constructed in the Meadows where 'Meadowlands' now is, and there we were led in groups each day after 12 noon. Our dinners were very good indeed and imagine my surprise when my very first meal was served to me by my Aunt Jane. Our meals were collected and served by monitors, each of us taking turns for this duty, and as the monitors were the last to get their dinner an extra dollop of something (usually custard with the sweet) was handed out. There was much jostling for the job of monitor. Then there was the 'school nurse' who visited us periodically to examine us. This entailed submitting to a close examination of our hands, eyes, ears, mouth and hair, the latter being ruffled and painstakingly scrutinised for 'nits'. I remember this lady as a young, dark haired, stern looking person with a pale complexion and wearing a brown uniform and hat who was really very kind. Her name was Nurse Stone and she was a regular visitor to every school in Tavistock as well as the welfare clinic in West Street where mothers went to collect their National Dried Milk and Virol for the little ones. Virol was a sort of thick syrup, light brown in colour and rich in vitamins. It tasted vile but was administered mercilessly by my mother every morning to me and my sister Dilys. It was supposed to 'do us good'.

The School Dentist visited annually and was a feared man. We children went as a class to the 'Old Grammar School' at the bottom of Plymouth Road (now a recreation centre) where the dentist had one of the seemingly enormous rooms to practice in. Our first visit was for an inspection and about a week later we would again attend for treatment. As you can imagine the first ones to go returned with bloodcurdling accounts of their sufferings which were reinforced as we awaited our turn by yelps from within the treatment room. There were no anaesthetics given for fillings, only for extractions, and the victims clung desperately to the arms of the chair trying to maintain a courageous silence whilst the whirring drill did its work. I recall one boy who fled the scene hotly pursued by his mother and the dental nurse and dragged back to the dreaded chair. I also recall how you were labelled a 'cissy' if your mother attended at all. I once had five teeth extracted in one sitting and went back to my class and continued my lessons as usual.

When I was nine, I and my classmates left Mrs Dunstan's class to the next class up with another lady teacher whose name I cannot remember. There we were taught 'double writing' which, when mastered, made us feel very grown up. Our new teacher believed in incentives for good efforts and a little red star would be stuck to the top corner of our written work to indicate her approval when we did well. Sometimes an extra endeavour was rewarded with a double star, which we would proudly display to our friends. She also presented a book prize each term out of her own pocket for the best performing pupil, but most of us realised there were far more clever people to contend with in the class and that for us it would be a hopeless task to come out top so we contented ourselves with the occasional star.

It was about this time we were given advance notice of the so-called 'Scholarship Exam' we would be taking the following year; those who passed would go to Tavistock Grammar School.* For most of us it was an opportunity we did not at the time appreciate but which our parents were delighted about, egging us on to do our very best with wild promises of being rewarded with bicycles should we succeed. Some of us did succeed and got their bikes – others did not. Anyhow there was an air of expectation hanging over us from this time on.

* *This exam was afterwards replaced by the '11 Plus' which became the only way into the Grammar Schools. Our group were the last to sit the Scholarship.*

Incidentally girls were not admitted to this particular school until 1932. After passing the exam they (only girls not the boys) underwent an interview to assess their 'suitability'. My cousin Cora Doidge, who not only passed the exam but was top of her class, failed the interview and was never told the reason. She came from a modest home with working class parents.

Another activity we undertook at least twice a week was PT and our supervisor was a fit looking man with a gruff voice called Gregory. The girls exercised separately and I do not know who their instructor was. We ran 'on the spot', did press ups, arm stretching, etc., under his critical eye. If we slacked he would suddenly appear with a whack of his hand on our ear (yes, we did see stars!). For all that, he commanded a lot of respect for dedication and even-handedness (no pun intended!). Mr Gregory was also a talented artist whose water colour paintings were often exhibited in the town. He would take an art class occasionally and demonstrate how things should be done by pinning a sheet of paper to an easel and drawing and painting a picture as we watched. I often met him in later life when he was always the first to extend greetings in a friendly manner to which I was pleased to respond in kind. He lived in one of the little row of terraced cottages at the top of Old Launceston Road.

My final year at Council School was spent in Miss Callaway's class. She was an elderly and very experienced teacher, who it was my good fortune to have. A strict no nonsense disciplinarian, she was also very kindly and committed, taking a personal interest (so it seemed) in each one of us. Most of our lessons consisted of elaborating and extending the lessons we had already learned in preparation for The Exam but it was not all sweating away at academic subjects – far from it. We formed a percussion band once every week with a kettle drum, recorders, cymbals, and of course triangles. Simple music sheets bore the easy to understand notes in different colours for each instrument; when we got going and after some practice I believe the results were quite pleasing. Like all the boys I craved a turn with the kettle drum but it was not to be – that honour was always reserved for Gerald Dunstan. Miss Callaway was also a masterful story teller who entertained us greatly with her interpretation of 'The Wind in the Willows' among other stories. She imitated each character to perfection and held us entranced.

There was a tragedy in Miss Callaway's class which I have never forgotten. John Foan was an orphan and lived in the orphanage for boys at the junction of Spring Hill and Ford Street. It was always known as the 'Scattered Home' and my understanding was the boys were well cared for. I remember them walking to school in twos, supervised by one of the older lads, all of them wearing grey trousers, grey pullovers, grey socks and nailed boots. John sat next to me in class but one Monday morning he failed to appear. He had been killed falling from a 'conker tree'. Mr Bucknell informed the class of this in a kindly, straightforward manner and warned us boys to be very careful when 'conkering' and to watch out for rotten branches (the dead boy had stepped on one and it snapped causing him to fall to his death). We were not told never to climb trees again; we did not receive counselling; we did not fling our arms around one another sobbing.

John died unnecessarily because there used to be a huge conker tree on the front lawn of the Vicarage. It was forbidden to approach this tree or collect fallen conkers but if you went to the front door and rang the bell and asked politely, a servant maid would fill your open palms with conkers taken from a sack full of them that was kept in the porch just for that purpose. It was an exercise in good manners initiated by the then Vicar of Tavistock, the Rev. Bickersteth.

One day our headmaster entered the class and went for us 'hammer and tongs' for slacking in our studies. In my case it was probably deserved but he made the mistake of pointing out one or two other pupils who he said would pass The Exam with flying colours and named them as an example to us all. Well, the big day arrived at last and with some trepidation we took our places and were issued with the exam paper. To my surprise there were not the number of sums I expected; instead there were general knowledge questions and simple common sense ones such as: *Postmen wear blue uniforms. This man is wearing a blue uniform, therefore he must be a postman. True or false?'* Some weeks later Mr Bucknall again came into our class and called out six or seven names of which mine was one. My first reaction was 'what have I done this time?' but when we got to his office he was all smiles. 'You have passed the Scholarship' he said, 'and all the others have failed. Well done'. We returned to our classroom to find one of those he had previously named as certain to pass crying bitterly having failed after all. His name was Robin Pook and he was certainly one of the brightest ones in our group. Apart from feeling a little guilty about my own success I have felt ever since that exams are not the best way of assessing someone's abilities and that a continuing monitoring of day to day term work is not only more fair, but more accurate. The rest of the class, which included some of my best friends whom I had known from infancy, prepared to go to Dolvin Road Secondary Modern School whilst we basked in the exhilaration and delight of our parents for days afterwards and wondered what awaited us after the summer holiday when we would start attending Tavistock Grammar School.

Classmates

Among my 'Council School' contemporaries were:

Trevor Saundry: My best friend and a Plymothian. His family lived in Tavistock for the duration of the war. He and his brother Barry were firm friends throughout their stay. Sadly Trevor died just as this document was completed.

John Greening: His father was a builder and John followed him in the business. John's favourite stunt was to rub his eyes vigorously and suddenly open them when his eyelids would be inside out to reveal his staring eyeballs surrounded by circles of red. The girls would run off screaming leaving us laughing. He and I were great friends and I regret not ever meeting him in adult life.

Tony Palmer: He lived in the house facing Vigo Bridge by the mini-roundabout. He was a pale faced lad with dark hair, thoroughly nice and a quiet friendly person. His life ended tragically many years later.

John Davies: A quiet industrious boy who lived in the last house at the Abbey Bridge end of Dolvin Road called 'The Shack'. I met him again when I was home from sea when he fixed my grandmother's gas light as an employee of the Gas Board as it then was.

Roger Verrall: He was living with his grandparents, Mr and Mrs C. Ham, who lived in one of the two houses in Kilworthy Hill, next to what is now the 'Ordulph Arms'. Charlie Ham was for many years the Porter at the Bedford Hotel. Roger's home was in Southampton and he was sent to Tavistock because of the bombing raids there. Roger was brainy and later joined the R.A.F. as an Officer Cadet at Cranwell despite having a stammer. It was a proud achievement.

Mervyn Stoneman: We both worked for the *Tavistock Times* in later life. I was very sorry to learn of his death fifty years later from a nephew of his.

Margaret Rogers: Lived in Chapel Street and left us to go to Miss Balkwell's School. She was in my class again at Grammar School. Her grandfather and my grandmother were cousins.

Glenda Roberts: She was my cousin (her mother and mine were sisters) and a playmate all through our childhood. Her parents lost their home at Crownhill early in the war after a direct hit by a German bomb in the blitz after which they took refuge in Tavistock and remained there for the rest of their lives.

Audrey Peters: She was in the same ward as me at Tavistock Hospital having undergone the same operation I had for Peritonitis. We were both just over three years old.

Marie Chalmers: Was also in the same ward for exactly the same operation as Audrey and myself; must be a record. I always exchanged greetings with both girls whenever we met.

PLYMOUTH ROAD SCHOOL

Opened in 1856 by the British Society, which represented the interests of the Nonconformist Churches, the school housed here emerged finally as a County Primary School. It moved to Crowndale in 1991, after which the building became a doctors' surgery.

TAVISTOCK TOWN COUNCIL

Commemoration Plaque for Plymouth Road County Primary School (known as the 'Council School').

Christine Stevens: A playmate before and after starting school. She lived just two doors away at The Lawn, Brooklands. When she got older she developed a beautiful singing voice. I believe she married a Curate.

May Penhall: A quiet girl who not only was in my class at school but attended the Congregational Church for Sunday School as I did.

Margaret Cornish: She was my dancing partner every time we had country dancing at primary school. She was a friendly delightful girl who lived in Pixon Lane and I was very sorry to hear she has now passed away.

Eric Giles: Another playmate of mine before and after starting school. He lived in one of the flats at Brooklands House and was a gentle happy boy who in adult life very appropriately joined the Church of England priesthood.

Brian Hicks: A thoroughly good natured and happy individual. Brian lived in one of the 'Duke of Bedford' cottages in Parkwood Road and we were friends up until we both left school. We never met again but I would like to think he did well.

Paddy Dunne: He too lived in a flat at Brooklands House – the one immediately above mine. His older sister Marion was in the W.R.N.S. during the war.

Tony Jope: For some reason Tony was in the 'enemy' camp which opposed our 'gang'. All without malice of any kind, just good fun and we were in truth good pals. His home was approached by double iron gates and some steps in Parkwood Road before the entrance to Brooklands. This entrance served two large houses at the top of two long sloping gardens. There was also entry from Exeter Street which was closer to the rear of the house and therefore most used.

The 'Council School' today, now a doctor's surgery. (Author's photo)

Henry Knott: A big lad whose parents were both small in stature. Like me Henry was always getting into scrapes and his mother, who was a very kindly gentle soul, worried a lot about him. He went to work and live in north Devon early in life.

Margaret Crocker: She lived at the top of Rix Hill and was a delightful young girl with black hair, round-faced and always smiling.

There were many others I can recall by appearance but whose names I have forgotten and I apologise to them for that. Although we all had our childish arguments at times there was not one enemy among them and I have only pleasant memories of our times together.

Schools (Part 2)

The year 1945 was a momentous one. In May the German war ended, followed by the Japanese surrender in August. Best of all for me, it was the year my father came home for good. He was a Chief Yeoman of Signals in the Royal Navy, whose twenty-one years service was completed in 1942, but of course he could not be discharged with a war on, and so consequently he served a total of twenty-five years 'man and boy'. It was also the year I started at Tavistock Grammar School.

A new world opened to me, a world where the masters and mistresses wore gowns; where we boys were called by our surnames but girls retained their Christian names; where there were prefects and detentions; where I was brought into contact with girls and boys from other parts of the district (Princetown, Mary Tavy, Sydenham Damerel, Crapstone, and Dousland among others) and in some cases from more prosperous families. We were issued with a programme detailing which lessons we were to attend and which classroom they would be held in – with homework to do each evening. We wore a school uniform for the first time too. Boys had black blazers with the Tavistock Coat of Arms badge and black caps which bore the same insignia. A black and red striped tie and grey trousers completed the outfit (I believe the same uniform is worn today by pupils of Tavistock Comprehensive School). Younger lads had short trousers and graduated to long ones usually in the second year in accordance with the fashion of those days. The girls wore white blouses and black tunics with a red sash around their waists, red blazers and black berets with the school badges. During the summer months a white and black chequered dress replaced the tunics, and very smart they looked.

Mr J. Whitfield was the headmaster when I first attended that school. He was the most immaculately turned out man I ever saw. He set off from the headmaster's house in Woburn Terrace each morning at ten minutes to nine for the short walk to school, always at a brisk pace across the little bridge between the tennis courts and the Sir Francis Drake bowling green and along the side of the Tavistock canal. He usually wore a dark blue suit and always carried a briefcase. Mr Whitfield was a mild mannered man but very strict and when he entered our dining room for lunch an immediate hush ensued. I sat next to him at table several times and found him a very amiable person who was interested not only in us but was familiar with our parentage too. How he came to know so much I never ascertained but he knew my father was an artist and was most interested to learn what he was painting at that moment. A year or so after my entry he left to become headmaster of a boy's private school (or so I was told) and 'Spot' Hartley, our Senior Master, took over. After an interval, Mr Whitfield's successor Mr K. D. Anderson arrived. He had been a Major in the army and brought a military flavour with him without the brusqueness usually associated with officer types then. His wife taught us English and Biology and sometimes so

The Grammar School Art Room as I remember it. (Courtesy Tavistock History Society)

did he. They had two young children. I recall Mr Anderson as a kindly, homely man without a trace of malice in him.

The Assembly Hall, with a large art room above it, dominated the centre of the school and was encircled by a stone cloister. On the outside periphery of the cloister the individual classrooms were situated and included two much larger than the rest that contained mahogany benches for physics, chemistry and biology lessons. On the benches there were a number of Bunsen burners and a selection of small glass bottles arranged in neat groups, containing a fascinating array of brightly coloured liquids. On one occasion our teacher was called away for a short time and two or three of us boys took advantage of her absence to 'experiment'. A little of each bottle's contents were put into a test tube and heated. A thick evil smelling green gas quickly permeated our classroom and invaded the cloisters outside. It was the only time I saw Mr Anderson visibly angry and rightly so. Our class was banned from the science room for the rest of that term.

We changed classrooms for every subject, each classroom being designated for a particular subject as well as the starting place for every day of each grade or 'form' as it was then called. Thus when the bell was rung to end a lesson the cloister was a crowded place with the mass movement of staff and pupils from one room to another. A one-way system prevailed and punishment was certain to follow any infringement of this rule.

Morning Assembly always followed the roll call held in class. There was a stage where the headmaster held sway and a grand piano beautifully played by Mrs Verrall, our music teacher, to accompany the hymn that always came after prayers. Then there would be announcements and sometimes a 'pep talk' before we dispersed for the first lesson of the day. At the beginning of the autumn term the headmaster read out the names of those who passed the School Certificate exam* and were invited to applaud them which we did. The hysterical shrieks of joy so prevalent today lay far in the future and would not have been tolerated anyway.

* *Designed for University Entry. To qualify you had to pass in at least five subjects, English and Maths being compulsory, together with a Science subject and two others of your choice. There were no second chances; failure in one subject meant you did not get a certificate.*

I believe Mrs Verrall was more than just a music teacher, having been a professional musician and singer who often gave us impromptu recitals which were a joy to hear. Many of the lovely melodies I learned from her are firm favourites of mine today, some of them Schubert compositions which she sang in German. Her lessons were held in the assembly hall and because of its central location her music resounded throughout the school, sometimes distracting us but always a pleasure to listen to – at least to me.

I possessed a favourable soprano voice and was sometimes chosen to perform solos. A regular event was the annual Tavistock Drama Festival held in our assembly hall. We pupils were encouraged to enter one of the many musical and drama competitions but my encouragement came from my father who never asked what was open to me only what the set piece was, it being taken for granted I would enter. One year I took part in the music section rendering 'Where E're You Walk' (Handel) as a solo with piano accompaniment. I was first on and nervous, the result being I did not qualify for a place in the top three who received certificates. I made up for it next time by coming first in Elocution by reciting the well-known poem *The Tiger* by William Blake ('Tiger, tiger burning bright' etc.). My Dad drilled me for weeks and was afterwards informed by the Adjudicator who judged the several entries that although my diction was not quite as it should be he was impressed by the spirit I imparted into the piece. 'Reciting the lines with beautifully pronounced English is all very well' he told him, 'but the essence of the poem was captured to perfection by your son which is why I gave him top marks'. How proud my father was, but no-one else even said 'well done' because staff and pupils alike expected a girl entrant who took elocution lessons to win hands down, and I think on reflection I spoilt her day and theirs. I have the certificate to this day and revere it in my father's memory. The same thing almost occurred the next year at the Launceston Drama Festival held in Launceston Town Hall. On this occasion 'Sennacharib' ('The Assyrian came down like the wolf on the fold' etc.) by Lord Byron was delivered by about ten entrants. I had been feeling unwell that morning and when my turn came all went according to plan until I forgot my lines and had to be prompted. It often happens but there was an automatic deduction of ten points and that cost me a winning place.

The art room above the hall was also my first classroom (Form 1A) under our art teacher Miss Field. I remember her as a young, dark haired, very pleasant lady who lived in Parkwood Road and cycled to and from school in all weathers. I enjoyed and was good at art which was confined to painting (watercolours) and drawing, some of my contributions being exhibited on the classroom wall together with other pictures far more talented than mine. During that first year I was introduced to subjects none of us 'Council School' entrants had ever heard of: Geometry for example, Algebra, Biology

The Grammar School, Tavistock

Tavistock Grammar School as I remember it. Now a Primary School.

and Physics. It was a struggle but I must have done reasonably well because I retained my 'A' Form status in my second year. Incidentally the above mentioned subjects were not unknown to the girls and boys who did their basic learning at Miss Balkwell's school, an indication of the very high standard that prevailed there.

Our sports facilities were very good indeed. There were approx. five acres of playing fields and a pavilion equipped with changing rooms and showers. We played cricket, hockey, and football (the girls played tennis, hockey and basketball). I have heard it said the boys played rugby but that was not the case. We all practised athletics which were put to the test in the summer term when a Sports Day was held. For this event a full size running track was marked out which incorporated markers for the 100 yards sprint, 220 yards, 440 yards (one lap), and the mile (four laps). Then there were the hurdles, discus and javelin throwing competitions, long jump, high jump and the hop-skip-and-jump (referred to as the 'triple jump' these days) all of which were undertaken to raucous cheers by members of the four 'Houses' we were allocated to. My House was Glanville and we congregated in a classroom once a week for morning prayers instead of Assembly and discussed various matters, such as appointing the captains of various teams for all the sports and swimming competitions and organising strategies to beat our rivals. The other Houses were Drake, Bedford and Tremayne and competition was fierce. We were permitted to use the school equipment to practice with during our lunch breaks until one day someone misjudged throwing a javelin and it hit a boy who was watching and penetrated his calf, leaving a neat hole which, strangely, did not bleed a lot. That terminated our lunchtime practice sessions – that boy could easily have been killed.

Every year there was compulsory cross-country running for us boys. There was a senior run of approx. five miles and a junior one which was approx. three miles. We started off from Drake Statue and raced away past the Roman Catholic Church and up Crease Lane to Lumburn where we turned down another smaller lane and across a stream before making our way over some fields to the Tavistock canal. The juniors joined the canal tow path at Crowndale for the run home, finishing at the road bridge by Drake Statue. The seniors went further and joined Crowndale Road near Shillamill for the final stretch all the way to the school entrance near West Bridge. I remember running down some of the lanes overgrown with stinging nettles and brambles, before crossing a stream which was too wide to jump with the result that most of us were a sorry sight on our return, mud splattered, wet and bleeding from multiple scratches. We didn't care – and, in any case, it attracted attention (and some admiration) from the girls. My three cousins, Bill, John and David Doidge were all good runners and sportsmen. One year Bill won the senior cross country race and his brother John won the junior event. A year or so later their younger brother David did the honours in the junior race.

Outstanding sportsmen I recall were a prefect called 'Freddie' Evans who threw the discus in classic style; 'Bob' Pate who was a truly first class batsman in the first eleven cricket team together with another prefect, a tall lanky lad called Pudifoot who bowled like a professional. There was my future brother-in-law Ron Marks, a hard hitter at the batting crease. Ron had the distinction of achieving what every Grammar School batsman wanted to do – he hit the pavilion clock. The line of the pitch made the clock an irresistible challenge to batsmen on the 'on' side and during an inter-school match he hit a 'skier', which smashed the glass front but luckily left the clock intact and in working order. In my own age group there were boys who were good 'all rounders'– Brian Hicks, Polkinhorne (a tall fair-haired lad from Bere Alston nicknamed 'the octopus' because he had long arms and was a natural goalkeeper), Ken Newnham, and Danny Gliddon, among others. My cousin John Doidge, previously mentioned, was the hero of the school one year when he won no less than seven events on sports day, mainly running. Our cricket teams played away and at home to Kelly College, Devonport High School for Boys, and Dartmouth Royal Naval College among others but never Dolvin Road School which was on our doorstep and had boys of equal ability to our own. My cousin John tells me Dolvin Road was later added to the list of opponents, and quite right too.

Great emphasis was placed on 'sportsmanship'. Some of us boys had never taken part in organised games and had much to learn. My first game of football, for example, was supervised by 'Dicky' Dymond, an elderly little man much respected by us all. My friend Brian Hicks was centre forward and I was inside left. Brian said, 'what do I do when he blows his whistle?' 'Kick the ball to me and I'll kick it back and we'll take it from there', I replied. In no time the ball was being vigorously pursued by every lad on the field including our own goalkeeper in the other side's penalty area trying to score! Poor old 'Dicky' despaired of us but at last he managed to impart to us the principles of playing as a team, in which respect may I add, he was always adamant that the individual who scored a goal was not to be patted on the back or made to feel clever. 'It is a team effort' he would say, 'and it is the team who have scored'. How right he was. I cannot imagine what he would have thought of today's players jumping up and down like six-year-olds because they have scored a goal or won a game – or perhaps I could.

The same gentleman took us for our first 'proper' game of cricket. We not only learned the approved methods of batting and bowling but, as before, he insisted on the appropriate courtesies being observed. An incoming batsman for example would receive quiet applause in recognition of his (supposed) ability no matter what he scored. This was extended to every player who was dismissed even if he scored a 'duck' because it was always understood how much better he might have done. When the game finished the entire 'home team' stood in line outside the pavilion and clapped their opponents in and this applied to football and hockey games too. John Doidge once got a reproach he never forgot from 'Spot' Hartley (Senior Master), for not raising his cap in acknowledgement for the applause he got at the end of a game for being top scorer.

Youngsters of today may smile at these niceties but the present day dogma of 'win at any cost' had not yet afflicted us. We believed that if you could not win fair and square it was not worth the trouble. It was more than that though, because it also taught us restraint and good manners. We all did our very best for our school but if we lost, it was because the other side were better than us on that occasion and no excuses were made. We would have been appalled had we seen then the antics of so-called sportsmen now hugging and kissing, jumping up and down like toddlers, waving their fists, turning somersaults, tearing off their shirts to wave at the crowds, spitting and cursing like troopers, and receiving more adulation than they deserve simply for playing a game. Arguing with the referee or cricket umpire was unthinkable – even the shaking of head after an lbw decision would have brought a reproach.

There were very few bullies at the Grammar School, but there was one in particular whom I will simply call 'R' who thought he was tough but was really just a loud mouthed ruffian who took pleasure in pushing younger, smaller boys around. Such people usually get their desserts in the end and he got his. He had been given a new bicycle for his birthday but when he went to get it after school he found it was suspended from the bicycle shed roof with what seemed like miles of wire wrapped around it. Wire was interspersed around the spokes of the wheels, all around the handlebars, chain, pedals, everything. How it was ever untangled I will never know. The following morning after assembly the boys were told to stay behind by our Senior Master who had a reputation for strictness. He came straight to the point by referring to the bicycle incident and inviting those responsible ('if they were man enough') to own up and take their punishment. There was a scraping of chairs as the culprits leapt to their feet to be recognised (and secretly admired by their colleagues). I never discovered what their fate was but 'R' stood at the master's side crying and blubbering like a baby. I was told years afterwards he joined the South African Police.

At thirteen years of age we became eligible to join the school Army Cadet Force. Most of the boys elected to join and what a marvellous time we had going on parade every Friday morning, undergoing training in rifle drill, shooting at Shillamill Ranges, learning map reading and field craft, and of course the annual camp. We wore our uniform with pride and my first camp was under canvas ('bell tents' – six to a tent) on Salisbury Plain, not far from Warminster. We watched regular soldiers demonstrating various weapons from Lee Enfield rifles to Bren Guns, Sten guns, Mortars and Bazookas. We witnessed the awe inspiring fire power of anti-tank guns on redundant tanks and lorries and were amazed to see thick steel plating twisted like chewing gum with bullet holes straight through them. We quaked under the thunderous noise of tanks revving their engines over the horizon before racing into view with flame throwers blazing. We took part in a guard mounting competition when selected cadets 'bulled' their boots and shined their brasses and badges in readiness for a display of marching and rifle drill under the eye of no less a person than Regimental Sergeant Major R. Brittain of the Coldstream Guards. This man stood well over six foot tall, with a huge girth and a fierce moustache. He was renowned for possessing the 'loudest voice in the British Army' but we found him to be a disappointment in this respect when he supervised the morning parades, screaming commands in a long drawn out falsetto voice like a woman's. On one occasion though I was within earshot when he was talking to some senior officers in a deep growl and realised, here was a man to be reckoned with after all.

Meals were prepared in the open on 'field kitchens' and certainly did not resemble home cooking but we didn't care; it was all part of soldiering to us even though we washed the greasy tin plates and mugs we were issued with in buckets of cold water and wiped them clean with bunches of grass. Buckets of cocoa were laid out between the rows of tents each night and we dipped our mugs in last thing before 'Lights Out'. We were woken by the band and bugles of the Durham Light Infantry, our hosts, marching up and down between the rows of tents in the early dawn. It was education of a very special kind and I would not have missed it for anything in this world. Our CO was Major W.C. Rawling, a mathematics teacher, and he deserves full credit for enthusiasm.

To return to schooling proper: our academic studies were expanded in Form 2A to include French and Latin. In my second year I caught chicken pox which kept me in isolation at home for almost a month. When I returned to school I learned that in my absence Mr Rawling had asked where 'Jammy' was. The name stuck and for the rest of my schooldays I was known as and called 'Jammy' James. Then my father developed the first symptoms of Hodgkin's disease which killed him after eighteen months of agony and suffering. My school work suffered accordingly and I am sorry to say not only did I fall far behind but failed to appreciate the extra attention I got from some members of staff to enable me to catch up. The result was that when I entered my third year I was relegated to Form 3B.

It should be explained there was a two tier system at that school. The bright pupils who would maintain the school's reputation for good School Certificate results were retained in the 'A' stream where they benefited from the attention of the senior and best teachers; the rest were abandoned to the 'B' stream where they were taught by less qualified or able staff, but those who did well could be reinstated to the 'A' stream at the start of the new academic year the following September.

My father died towards the end of my second year and my learning hit an all time low, with the result that I was downgraded to the 'B' stream as already mentioned. Our 3B form teacher was a mild mannered, kind and gentlemanly man called Pearce who was inevitably dubbed 'Tom'. He was a tall man, very fit but balding and wore large thick-rimmed glasses. He took me aside one day and gave me the most encouraging talk I ever had. 'James' he said, 'you are not fulfilling yourself or your abilities. You could do well if you really tried and I want to see you way up in my class near the very top'. I was inspired and from that moment stopped feeling sorry for myself and set out to do my best and show what I was made of. It paid off. At the end of our summer term we had exams and the results, together with our half term and full term progress, were announced before the summer holidays and recorded on a written report for our parents to read. The day this took place, Mr Pearce leaned over his elevated desk and looked down at us to read out the results. His face was beaming as he started with me: 'James – first, first and first'. There was a gasp from the class and I felt ten foot tall.

Here I must again digress and explain just what kind of institution the Grammar School then was. The attitude in general was one of superiority and was steeped in the 'old boy' tradition; indeed one of our masters often referred to an individual as 'old boy'. Let me give some examples. One morning at Assembly a master had this to say: 'I have had a number of complaints from members of staff concerning the manner in which they are greeted out of school. There is only one way in which this should be done. Firstly the boys will doff their cap – you will not touch the peak of your cap like a taxi driver expecting a tip. Secondly all pupils will then use the following phrase "Good Morning Sir" or Mrs/Miss as the case may be followed by their name. May I remind you this is Tavistock Grammar School, not the sort of institution situated at the other end of the town', waving his arm in the direction of Dolvin Road. As a matter of fact the Dolvin Road School had an enviable reputation for good manners among the population of Tavistock. In any case, I personally did not share his view at all because many of my best friends attended there and they were the nicest boys I knew. The same man constantly went out of his way to look for misdemeanours to punish. He wore heavy shoes with protective tacks in the soles and you could hear him coming along the cloistered corridors with his distinctive 'click-clack' sound. Everybody froze in their seats until he had passed by for he always glanced through the classroom windows to see what was going on, and any sign of restlessness or inattention was sure to bring him to a halt. He would enter the classroom, apologise to the teacher for the interruption, and say something like, 'That boy there! Come and see me at four o'clock!' when you knew you would be for it. I once had an argument with a girl after class which resulted in some sharp exchanges and a door being slammed shut leaving me in class and the young lady marching defiantly away. The incident came to the attention of this same man who cornered me to ask what was going on. I told him I'd had an argument and lost my temper. 'Who with?' I was asked. 'I'd rather not say Sir'. 'I see – then you would prefer to take the punishment yourself?' 'Yes', and punishment was duly awarded. I discovered later the same interview had taken place with the other party who had likewise declined to name her argumentative opponent (me). She too received punishment. There was never any mercy or mitigating circumstances as far as this individual was concerned; he maintained a reign of terror and never smiled.

My brother-in-law Ron Marks was a talented sportsman and played football, cricket and hockey for the school. When he was just fourteen-years-old he was selected to play for Tavistock in a football match, but as the date clashed with a school team hockey match he went in a straightforward manner to see the headmaster and ask his permission. Not only was this refused but he got a stern lecture on 'loyalty' to his school and was awarded a hundred lines on the same theme. He ended up playing hockey for the school as arranged but imagine the credit the school would have received had one of their boy pupils, only fourteen years of age, played for his home town's football team.

On another occasion one of our masters was suffering from a bad liver or some other complaint and took it out on us. 'I don't know how some of you people got into this school' he raved, after which he slammed into us for a good five minutes, reducing one boy to tears. He happened to be a bright pupil and was very well spoken. Our tormentor sensed he had gone too far and actually put his arm around him murmuring, 'There, there, old chap. You mustn't take it too hard'. The same man never forgot to set us homework and to give him his due he went through it at the next lesson when we marked our own books and called out the score afterwards. One boy called out 'Three sir!' after one session upon which the master in question sighed audibly before remarking 'Only three out of a possible ten? But then, your father is just a butcher isn't he' (the father was a well respected and well liked tradesman in Tavistock). His son was big enough to have given that man a thrashing, and looking back I am surprised he did not. Another time he told me it was about time I learned to talk 'properly', referring to my Devonshire accent. The lamentable thing was he himself did not speak what he called 'properly' as he pronounced his words with a twang I have not identified to this day, but it was far from posh. In any case, most of us retain at least a trace of our regional accent which goes a long way to make up our English heritage and is nothing to be ashamed of.

As recently as 2005 a cousin of mine referred to both these men as sadists. I regard them as little men who basked in a little world like so many petty tyrants of those times. I will not name them for the sake of their families who may still reside in the area – those who were there will recognise them. I believe it was largely their influence which prevented me from being reinstated to the 'A' stream after doing so well. On the first day of the next academic year, my '4B' class was visited by pupil messengers naming those who were promoted to the upper class and naturally I awaited the summons but it never came. I was to be a 'B' pupil for the rest of my schooldays. My feeling was it did not matter how hard I tried, I would never prove my worth so I never bothered again. I became notorious for getting into scrapes, not doing any homework, and generally not caring about anything except the day I would be free to leave. Years later, my children attended a similar Grammar School in Hampshire and experienced the very same attitudes from the staff as are related above. An air of superiority and prejudice prevailed which leads me to believe nothing has changed or is likely to.

The following members of staff live on in my memory:

Mr W. C. Rawling – Mathematics. He was elected to Tavistock Town Council and became a JP.

Mr C. Hartley – French. He was known as 'Spot' and was a renowned disciplinarian. On the wall of his classroom was a notice: '*Ici en Parle Française*' which meant everything

Tavistock Grammar School staff and pupils.

was conducted in French and God help you if you opened your book at the wrong page when instructed.

'Taffy' Davis – English.

Mr Barnes – Mathematics. He was very affable and caring man who transferred from Dolvin Road School.

Mr Charleston – Geography and Games. He was an Anglo-Indian of a pleasant disposition who became very popular.

Mr F. ('Freddie') Wrench – Physics and Chemistry. A bluff Yorkshireman who kept a rubber Bunsen burner tube coiled on his desk. He called it 'his tame red snake' and it was applied to the backsides of boys who misbehaved – the humiliation hurt more than the beating.

Mr Pearce – Mathematics. He was a mild mannered man who was highly respected. I was surprised to meet him in the local Liberal Club one day when he played billiards with me and gave me a sound thrashing without stunning or spinning the cue ball; it was all done with natural angled shots beautifully applied and I learned a lot about that game from him.

Mr Ibbotson – English. A dry old stick whose favourite stance in class was with his back against the radiator and both arms around two willing girls (I have marvelled since how he got away with it). On Saturdays he was often seen walking around Tavistock accompanied by two or three girl pupils. For all that he was quite harmless and was a good teacher at times.

Mr R. ('Dicky') Dymond – Geography and Religious Instruction. Who among those who were there does not remember this delightful gentleman who never raised his voice yet exercised perfect control? Anyone who distracted the class was politely but firmly asked to 'kindly leave the class and wait outside in the corridor'. In due course he would appear and ask if we had anything to say. He expected and always got a profuse apology whereupon the culprit would be permitted to rejoin the class. He had travelled extensively in his youth in Europe, Canada and the USA, and regaled us with tales about his experiences which we were enthralled by and learned a lot from. Dear old 'Dicky' deserves a chapter of his own.**

'Officer X' – Temporary teacher for French. He was a retired army officer of the old school, straight out of the *Bumper Book for Boys*. Iron grey hair and moustache, monocle, tweed jacket and a permanent scowl were his trademarks, together with a gruff voice and a lot of bluster. He nearly always invited us to do some 'private study' whilst he studied the daily newspaper.

Mrs Verrall – Music and sometimes French. She was a highly talented lady.

Miss Nicol – Latin. She had a twin sister who looked exactly like her. They both rode bicycles and were distinguishable only by the clothes they wore which were of different hues. The other Miss Nicol nevertheless had to put up with numerous greetings in the town from children she did not know.

Miss Gibbs – Biology.

Mrs Anderson – English and Biology.

Miss Atkin – PT. As well as the girls, she took us boys in our first year after which a master took charge. Miss Atkin wore a short blue skirt and blue panties and was fond of demonstrating handstands. You can imagine the undivided attention she got.

Miss Parr – PT and Games. She succeeded Miss Atkin.

*** Mr. Dymond is best remembered for demonstrating a new type of pen he acquired. 'Just look at this' he would say, 'a pen that requires no ink and has a ball point instead of a nib' scribbling away as he spoke. 'It's called a Biro and I have no doubt it will be the pen of the future'. What prophetic words they were but we had to wait to take our turn with it: this new instrument spoiled our handwriting we were told by the school heads and it was forbidden to use one at school for several years (it took almost as long for a ball point signature to be accepted on a cheque or indeed any legal document).*

Then there was an influx of younger men back from active service with the armed forces:

Mr Meigh – French. He was a dour man with an abruptness that probably stemmed from the war. 'I was in the mess up at Alamein' he once confided when asked.

Mr Wilkinson ('Wilkie') – History and Games. A tall, fair-haired man who kept discipline on the cricket pitch with whacks from a cricket bat on our posteriors (it really hurt). Any inattention resulted in a cricket ball being thrown at you with a shout of 'look out!' to give you a sporting chance of ducking.

Mr Gill – French and Games. He was a superb cricketer who played for Tavistock. I have never seen a man who could hit the ball as hard and as high as he did and expected you to catch it.

Mr Trefor Thomas – Woodwork and Art. He had been a tank gunner in the Eighth Army and was a talented sculptor. He was a true Welshman and a very popular teacher. He went out onto his front lawn one night and shot himself. He is sadly missed and kindly remembered today by those who were privileged to have known him.

Mr Charnley – Games and PT.
Some of the above names may have been incorrectly spelt and I apologise for that – memories fade after sixty years but I have done my best to avoid mistakes.

The school caretaker was a retired army man, Sergeant Dingley, whose wife assisted him. He was a short man with greying hair, a bushy moustache and a brusque manner. He delighted in discovering any wrongdoing, however trivial, and reported them to (quote) 'the 'Ead' with undisguised enthusiasm. As a result the miscreant would in time be summoned to that person's office to 'take his medicine' and consequently Mr Dingley's popularity was never very great. I recollect his retirement when the whole school assembled to witness a farewell speech from Mr Anderson interspersed with sniffles from a now subdued Sergeant holding a handkerchief to both eyes. It brought forth a scathing comment from the back of the hall: 'look at him scritchin' (crying) like a baby!' To be fair he and his wife did a good job keeping the school and the grounds in admirable order.

At one time my Aunt Edith supplied and operated a Tuck Shop which opened during break-times. She sold cakes and tantalising tit-bits, all homemade, together with coffee or soft drinks, the proceeds going to school funds. Her services were freely given (something most of us were unaware of at the time). School dinners were served at the 'Old Grammar School' in Plymouth Road (now the J. J. Alexander Centre) and very good they were. Our dining hall was a lovely old room with wood panelling and bare floorboards with high windows overlooking the front of the building. We ate at trestle tables and sat on wooden forms; monitors collected the meals from a hatch from whence the kitchen staff issued them. When Mr Whitfield was headmaster members of staff were expected to sit at the head of each table but after he left they congregated on one table which I thought was a retrograde step.

There were two big events in our school calendar. The first of these was Founders Day and I do not recall the date except that it was a summer event. On that day the

The 'Old Grammar School' now named 'J. J. Alexander Education Centre' after a former Headmaster. (Author's photo)

entire school was paraded in groups with the teaching staff clad in their gowns and mortar boards and coloured sashes draped around their shoulders denoting the subject and class of degree they held. It was an imposing sight. We then marched up Plymouth Road to the Parish Church for a service of thanksgiving and a lot of self praise. On one occasion a tall ginger haired prefect sang the well-known Negro spiritual 'Deep River' unaccompanied and in a bass tone that reverberated to every corner of the church. His name was Bawden and his father was a bass singer who often sang with my own father, a bass baritone, at concerts in Tavistock Town Hall. His was a star turn that day and I can hear him now sending out deep raw notes that the late world-famous Paul Robeson would have been proud of.

One Founders Day my friend 'Bill' Sargent and I decided we did not want to go. When the school began to assemble for the march to the church we climbed unobserved onto the bicycle shed roof which had a parapet that shielded us from view but from which we could see the main gate. Frequent bobbing of heads to ascertain whether or not the main body had left led to our being discovered. 'Those boys up there come down at once!' It was our woodwork master Trefor Thomas. 'I know you're up there – I've got a gunner's eye' (he had been a tank gunner in the Eighth Army). We got down and faced him after admitting the reason for being up there. 'Well I'm not going either but I have work to catch up on and you have no excuse. I am only going to say this once: you still have time to join the rest of the school if you hurry so be off!' We went off but not to rejoin the school; our destination was the Liberal Club for a game of snooker (see Leisure part 2). Bill lived at Mary Tavy and had to leave at a quarter to four to catch the school bus home; we went down the stairs and onto the street and nearly bumped into Mr Thomas! To this day I admire his quick reaction which was to walk past as if we did not exist but next morning we were sent for. Mr Thomas did not snarl reproaches at us – he simply said, 'You two should know I do not expect ever to have to turn a blind eye twice in an afternoon', and that was all he said. We apologised of course but went away shamefaced which was more effective in the long run than any punishment.

In December there was a carol service when once again the entire school marched to the Parish Church. I remember Miss Nicol drilling us for days beforehand for 'Adeste Fidelis' ('O Come All Ye Faithful') which was always rendered in Latin. I can recite it to this day.

At the end of the Autumn term, prior to the Christmas holiday, the whole school enjoyed a Christmas party in the assembly hall during which a number of recitals and musical solos were performed and one year a short play featuring the school itself and members of staff was enacted by pupils. I recall a senior boy called Eggins imitating Mr Dymond to perfection in the role of 'Mr Emerald' and brought the house down. No-one laughed more heartily than 'Dicky' himself. Another lad took the part of 'Mr Spanner' (Mr Wrench) amid roars of laughter. At the end of the proceedings everyone sang the first verse of that ancient song 'Widecombe Fair' with much emphasis on the opening lines 'Tom Pearce, Tom Pearce, lend me your Grey Mare'. Our very own 'Tom Pearce' accepted it as a compliment – which it was – and faced us all smiling with enjoyment.

The remainder of my Grammar School career was a series of academic failures that brought despair and some recriminations from my tutors. I really could not have cared less. The one subject I excelled in was English Language; when I sat the School Certificate examination** in my final year I was awarded a 'Distinction' in this subject, the only one in the school and was summoned to the headmaster's office, not for punishment this time, but for congratulations. This eventually led to my being accepted for training as a Junior Reporter on the now redundant *Tavistock Times* under its controversial Editor Mr E. A. Whitaker – but that is another story.

** *This one was the last examination of this kind. It was replaced by GCEs.*

I walked off the premises on my last day without a word of advice or a good luck wish from anyone. I felt no bitterness and was without ambition of any kind. My journey through life has led me to many parts of the world and in many situations, ranging from cabin boy on a small tanker tramping around the globe to Shift Engineer on a power plant in Saudi Arabia. I regret nothing, envy no-one, have a loving family and am content in my retirement. That surely is a measure of success in anyone's life.

Classmates

My Grammar School classmates are too numerous to mention but included the following who I knew well:

Bill Sargent: A close friend until we left school after which we only met once. I'm afraid we gave our teachers a hard time and on one occasion we were separated to opposite corners of the classroom. He lived at Mary Tavy and had to catch a school bus home each evening so was exempt from detentions.

Tavistock Grammar School girls. (Panora Ltd., London)

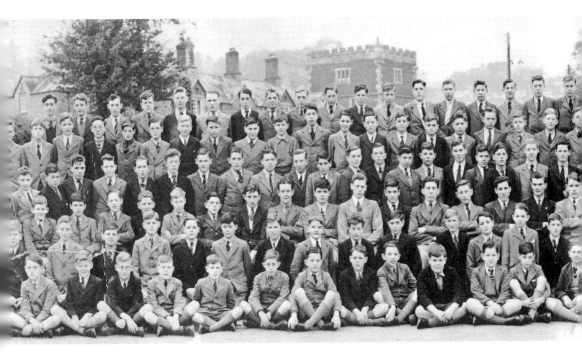

Tavistock Grammar School boys. Author third from left, second row. (Panora Ltd., London)

The late James ('Jimmie') Metcalf: We shared a desk in class until I was demoted to the 'B' stream. He lived in Princetown where his father was a Prison Officer at Dartmoor. We were all pleased for Jimmie when, in later life, he returned to Tavistock as headmaster of the Comprehensive School, and were saddened to hear he died so young.

Jim Parr: His father was a Colour Sergeant in the Royal Marines. He lived in Parkwood Road and, with several others from the area, became a good friend. He too shared my class for a while and afterwards joined the Royal Navy as a Writer. I was very sorry to hear he died in his sixties.

Peter Howell: Lived in the 'Round House' in Parkwood Road at the junction of that road with the turning to Wilminstone. What nice people his parents were, always welcoming and hospitable. Peter and I used to vie with each other as to who had the sharper creases in their trousers and the best shined shoes.

Danny Gliddon: Lived at 'The Lodge' to Mount House School where his father was Caretaker and Groundsman. Danny was a good all round sportsman and always good for a lark. We possessed make-shift catapults which were just rubber bands looped around our fingers and thumbs, but the paper pellets we fired were extremely painful when they struck (I speak from experience). It was my privilege to be Best Man at his wedding.

Maxwell Hayman: A cheerful lad who lived in a cottage at the top of Rix Hill. His mother was a remarkable and educated woman who could recite the 'Pied Piper of Hamelin' without hesitating and with perfect diction. Maxwell's father had served in the Royal Marines. Max joined the Royal Navy and we last met in the Newmarket Hotel in Bedford Square (now an estate agent's office) and enjoyed a couple of beers together with his shipmates. He was a Leading Signalman and doing well.

Alexander Townsend: His parents ran a newsagent shop in West Street. He was a late developer physically and retained a soprano voice long after his classmates' voices 'broke'. One of our masters used to ask a question in class and before anyone could answer would say in a booming tone, 'What's the answer Townsend?' upon which the expected titter of amusement would be heard. Yet Alexander was the proverbial 'knowledge box' who spent much of his spare time reading encyclopaedias. If there was an argument to be settled it was to Townsend we went and his word was accepted as final. Years later I was in Bedford Square when a tall, well built man came to my side saying 'Hello Trevor' in a deep manly voice. It was Alexander Townsend and I only wish that particular master could have been present.

Rupert Hill: Lived in Sydenham Damerel and, like me, got into a number of scrapes without doing anything really bad. I met him again more than fifty years later when he was an Officer at Dartmoor Prison.

'Bumbo' Bellamy: Came from a Peter Tavy farming family. His favourite act was to bare his stomach and invite you to hit him there as hard as you liked. Those who took up the offer never succeeded in hurting him and took great care not to return the compliment.

Also: **George Jewers, Rupert Davies, Alec Lavers, Leonard Lashbrook, John Palmer (previously mentioned), Eric Ball,** and **John Martin.**

Among the girls were: **Jean Redstone, Estelle Eggins, Glenda Roberts (my cousin), Angela Brooks, Avril Perkins, Kathleen Mitchell, Eleanor Griffiths, Marjorie Turner, Clara Toland,** and **Ruby Prout.** One of them was very special (she will know which one) and has never been forgotten.

There were many other boys and girls whose faces are familiar to me even now but whose names I cannot recall.

Grammar School Staff Photo

The staff of Tavistock Grammar School 1946. (Panora Ltd., London) They are (from left to right): Mr Ibbotson, Mr Gill, Mr T. Pearce, Mr W. Wrench, Mr R. Dymond, Mr Charnley, Mr W. C. Rawling, Mr Davis, Mr C. Hartley, Miss M. Nicol, Miss Gibbs, Unknown, Mrs Verrall, Unknown, Miss Parr, Miss Field, and School Secretary (name unknown).

'Remember The Sabbath Day, To Keep It Holy'

(Exodus Chapter 20 – The Ten Commandments)

Tavistock was a truly idyllic market town when I was a boy; unspoilt, orderly, trundling along happily in the old, old way. Everybody knew everybody else, if not individually then most certainly by family name, and keeping the family 'respectable' was a priority. As you can imagine there were several do's and dont's, especially in relation to the Sabbath.

On Sundays, no respectable woman would dream of putting out her washing to dry or indeed doing any washing at all, and every shop stayed firmly shut on that day. There were no sporting events either, although the cinemas opened on Sunday evenings and were always full. My grandfather disapproved of my going by remarking that the purpose of Sunday cinema was to provide somewhere for the soldiers to go to as an alternative to the pubs. I believe this concession was first introduced during the First World War when licensing hours were introduced for the same reason. The streets were deserted except when people congregated to go to church or chapel and when they came out afterwards there would be a babble of voices engaged in conversation – it was a social occasion in many ways and a pleasant one.

To the dismay of us children, the see-saw and the swings which occupied the space between what is now Meadowlands and the River Tavy were chained and padlocked from Saturday evening until Monday morning. On one occasion my cousin John Doidge had been selected to represent Tavistock youth in a running event at a special sports day and went to his headmaster to ask permission to practice on the Grammar School sports field on Sunday afternoons. He was met with a curt refusal, and told his place should be at church (my cousin was already a regular churchgoer). I recall one Sunday afternoon delivering a message to my gran on my way to the river for a swim. She spotted my rolled up towel and asked where I was going. When I told her she shook her head in disbelief muttering 'I don't know what your mother is thinking about' and other scathing remarks of disapproval. She and most other older women drew their curtains on that day, sat in the gloom, read the Sunday papers and prepared for Chapel.

The Salvation Army played a large part in the proceedings when they marched through Brook Street and Duke Street every Sunday afternoon with the band playing and banners waving. On Sunday mornings, without fail, they would assemble at various locations in Tavistock and hold a short open air service with their band accompanying the hymns and a person from the ranks delivering a brief sermon at the top of his or her voice. In the evenings, during the summer months, the entire group with the band would hold a full service in Bedford Square to a congregation of townspeople and, for a time, American soldiers who perched on the churchyard wall. In the winter the evening service was held at their hall half way up Kilworthy Hill.

Tavistock Parish Church prior to WW1. Note the railings which were removed during WW2. (Courtesy Tavistock History Society)

My grandparents were Unitarians and worshipped at the Abbey Chapel every afternoon during the winter and at evening service as well in the summer months. As a small child I often accompanied them and sat quietly on the cushioned 'kneelers' which were meant for just that purpose – kneeling for the prayers. Sometimes the sermon seemed longer than usual, and I suppose I got restless and caused heads to turn in our direction, because every so often my grandfather's hairy hand would descend and gently tweak my ear, after which of course I remained silent.

When I was about four years old my cousin Roger, who was older than me, would call and take me to the afternoon Sunday school at the Congregational Church. This beautiful church was situated on the north side of Duke Street next to the White Hart Hotel (now an estate agent's office). It boasted a very high steeple which was a landmark in Tavistock, and the first building you saw when entering the town from the Plymouth direction on the old Southern Railway line, as the train left the cutting and onto the embankment at Crowndale. Inside the church was an altar on a raised platform with rows of pews in front and a semi-circular gallery supported by stone pillars. All the woodwork, pews and altar rail etc., was of dark polished wood and always spotlessly clean – not a speck of dust anywhere. The floor was of red and blue coloured tiles. There were no stained glass windows and the pulpit and altar were very plain. When I returned to live in Devon after many years of absence I was dismayed to find the church had been demolished, and to this day I cannot understand how anyone would sanction destroying this beautiful building and replacing it with an ugly glass fronted box called an office block.

My first Sunday school was conducted by a very sweet old-fashioned lady called Mrs Elliot and was held in an alcove in the main church area where we all sat in a semi-circle

The site of the Congregational Church after demolition. (Courtesy Tavistock History Society)

on tiny chairs. All that was expected of us was to pay attention to Mrs Elliot's kindly words about God and recite the words 'God is Love' one at a time at the end of the proceedings. We learned about the Missionary work in the South Seas and when I asked our lady tutor what exactly they did I got a vehement reply that was almost frightening in its intensity: 'To teach the heathens about God!' she said heatedly and with wide glaring eyes. My imagination for years afterwards was of holy men immersed in hot cauldrons battling with fuzzy-haired black cannibals wielding sticks.

When we reached the age of about eight (I think) we graduated to one of the plain rooms with wood flooring at the rear of the building and took part in more conventional services. We underwent an advanced level of instruction where we learned the Parables and the works and sayings of Jesus under the guidance of Miss Dorothy Barratt. She was a tiny, pale-faced, bespectacled young woman with the kindest face I ever set eyes on and a personality to match. She was employed in Barclays Bank in West Street and was always immaculate in appearance. During Christmas 1944 she gave me a copy of the Bible suitably inscribed on the flyleaf and I have it still – it is a treasured possession. I met Miss Barratt again when I was seventy years of age and she was in her nineties. I told her who I was and that the Bible she gave me was still safe on my bookshelf at home. 'Yes I remember', she said, 'you were one of my little boys' all of which made me feel like a 'little boy' once more. The senior man, who I suspect was a lay preacher, was her father, also short in build but a giant in stature and a highly respected businessman in the town ('Bertie' as he was known, together with his wife, operated a grocery shop in Brook Street). Dear old 'Bertie' Barratt was to be seen scurrying all over Tavistock, recognised from a distance by his shock of white hair and the navy blue pinstriped suit he always wore. His greeting was the same every time: 'Hello young man!' he would say, whether you were nine, nineteen or twenty nine years old and always with a cheerful smile. I can see him now on a Sunday afternoon standing before us, hymn book shaking in his hand, red in the face, roaring in a deep bass 'Onward Christian Soldiers' or one of the many other stirring hymns we sang.

There were four special events at the Congregational during the year. The first of these was 'Anniversary Sunday'. I do not recall exactly what the anniversary date was but on that Sunday the place was packed. Every pew was full downstairs as well as the gallery seats. Parents, aunts and uncles, friends and associates, members of other denominations, all came to lend their support on this special day. Some of the older boys and girls were selected for recitations and were drilled Sunday after Sunday to get their piece just right. Every child had a platform seat, dressed in their very best attire and surrounded by floral decorations to the admiration of family and friends. The church resounded with the singing and the booming of the organ's deep accompaniment. A full-time Minister was in attendance not only to preach but also to introduce us one by one as we came forward to deliver our recitations, long or short. When we came out afterwards, there in the street outside parents, aunts and uncles, grandparents and most of those who attended were waiting to greet us with happy smiling faces and praise for our performance.

Then there was 'Toy Sunday' when we were all invited to sacrifice a toy or maybe a book or two for orphans and other needy children. Everything we brought was displayed in front of the altar when most of us youngsters from modest homes gazed with envy on the expensive offerings from those better off than ourselves. I do not recall many adults attending this particular service; it was mainly a children's event where we were lectured about the unprivileged boys and girls who would receive the items we donated, with a reminder about how glad we should be to have Mummies and Daddies and happy homes. For me it was a lesson in charity which I have never forgotten.

Harvest Festival came next in our annual calendar. What a sight it was to see the lovely floral arrangements that bedecked the altar and the display of every kind of fruit and vegetable. Again the church would be full to capacity and the good old harvest hymns – 'Come Ye Thankful People Come, Raise a Glorious Harvest Home' and 'We Plough the Fields and Scatter the Good Seed on the Land' – were sung with such gusto it echoed all the way down Duke Street and into Bedford Square.

I only recall one Christmas at the Congregational. It must have been early in the war and a children's party was held in one of the upstairs rooms behind the church proper. Father Christmas was in attendance, there were games and a magician who I well remember producing a handful of silver coins by simply scratching the lapel of my jacket. At the conclusion, every child received a present from the great man himself, resplendent in red with his huge white beard. My present was a Jack-in-the-Box, an amusing toy long out of fashion and a disappointment to me I must add. For the uninitiated, it comprised a brightly coloured box with a spring loaded top. When you released the catch to open the box a little brightly coloured figure rather like Punch popped out on a spring accompanied by a loud wail. To tell you the truth it frightened me and I never opened it again.

For some reason I cannot now remember I began attending the Abbey Chapel again. The Minister was a remarkable elderly lady called Mrs Phyllis Mary Martin but who always introduced herself as Mrs Edgar Martin. Unlike many women Ministers of today she retained her femininity. No jacket and clerical collar for her; an ankle-length pure white gown was her attire for services and what an inspiring figure she looked with her immaculately groomed hair and twinkling spectacles. To me she had the appearance of an Angel. Her sermons were not long but always informative, up to date in content and delivered in a gentle caring manner. She was a dedicated Pacifist (that took courage in a town like Tavistock with a war raging) and whether it was to taunt the good citizens of the town or through sheer inflexibility (she could be extremely obstinate) I will never know, but many services ended with the well-known hymn:

'Once to Every Man and Nation
Comes the Moment to Decide...'

This was sung to the tune of 'Deutschland Uber Alles' the German National Anthem. Of course passers-by heard it and relayed the fact all over the town, prompting the sort of comments you can imagine and others you may not. Her forthrightness and provocative personality surfaced one day in Madge Lane where she often passed the Roman Catholic Priest who lived in Watts Road. On her way to the town she encountered the Priest who remarked 'Good morning Madam. We really cannot go on meeting like this can we? And me not knowing your name'. 'I am Mrs Edgar Martin' she replied. 'And I am Father ____' he said 'but you may call me Father'. 'Indeed I will not' she declared, adding 'you are not my father'. I do not know what compromise was agreed but rest assured it was not Mrs Edgar Martin who gave way.

Mrs Martin was fond of children and I know she had a soft spot for me. Prior to the Scholarship Exam (mentioned in my schooldays section) she invited me to tea straight from school two days each week. Her true purpose was to give me extra tuition in subjects she considered essential for the exam with the emphasis on English and Arithmetic. I'm ashamed to admit my enthusiasm did not live up to her expectations but she persevered and I began to realise how very kind it was of her to take such an interest in me and tried to respond as she would have wished. Anyway, I did pass the exam and realised much later in life how valuable her help had been. Her interest in me extended to persuading me to read the lesson in chapel every Sunday. Naturally I found this an ordeal at first but gradually I became very proficient and the task gave me a great deal of confidence.

One day she came to our house to ask my father's permission for me to take the service as she had a severe throat infection which restricted her speaking to a whisper. He agreed of course, and at the age of ten I conducted the entire service that Sunday, announced the hymns, read two lessons and gave the sermon Mrs Martin had written for me. I received several messages of congratulation from the congregation and a whole paragraph in the *Tavistock Gazette* headed 'The Little Minister'. My headmaster Mr Bucknell was delighted. He summoned me to his office and told me how pleased and proud he was to learn one of his pupils had performed so well and that it was a compliment for our school. I hadn't thought about that but he was right.

There were prisoners of war in the Tavistock area from around 1944 onwards. First there were Italians, billeted I believe at Plaster Down, followed by German soldiers who were interned mainly at Willsworthy Camp near Lydford. I recall gangs of them shovelling snow from the pavements in the town during one winter. One day on my

RCH, 1945.

'Little Minister' At Abbey Chapel

When Mrs. Edgar Martin, Minister of the Abbey Chapel, Tavistock, awoke on Sunday morning at her home, "St. Edmunds," Courtenay Road, it was to discover that her voice had practically gone.

It became necessary to consider the service to be taken that evening, and Mrs. Martin had an inspiration. She sent for 10-year-old Trevor James. He is the son of Mr. George James, R.N., Chief Yeoman of Signals, and Mrs. James, of Brooklands (who were married at the Abbey Chapel) and grandson of Mr. C. Doidge, gardener at the Bedford Hotel and for 40 years a member of the Abbey Chapel.

Trevor, who attends Tavistock Junior School, at once agreed to announce the hymns and read the lessons. He felt less certain about reading the sermon, which Mrs. Martin had written out, partly because the " n's " and " r's " of Mrs. Martin were of an unfamiliar type to him. To meet this, Mrs. Martin went through her manuscript, altering every one of those two letters.

Came the evening, and Trevor announced the hymns and read the lessons beautifully. No less so the sermon which was on the words " Ye shall be my witnesses."

A visitor to the Church told Mrs. Martin " That boy read far better than many ministers and parsons do—you could hear every word he said." And Mrs. Martin has since had a letter from an Abbey Chapel member, congratulating her on the little minister's " excellent work.

Report of my 'Ministry' in the *Tavistock Gazette* 1945. (Original cutting)

way home from the Council School I paused outside the Congregational Church after noticing an unusual notice pinned to the notice board. 'Chopin/Beethoven/Mozart. Admission Free' it said. I had never heard those names before, and because my curiosity had been aroused and admission was free, I went in and took a seat in the gallery along with several Tavistock residents already there. To my surprise there were four German soldiers in uniform seated on the stage below with musical instruments including a grand piano, a cello and violins. Without any introduction or comments they proceeded to render selections by all three composers and I was entranced. The experience changed my life to some degree and I fell in love with the melodies I heard that day, played with professional skill and applauded with vigour by the audience. I owe those Germans a lot of gratitude for my lifelong love of the great composers.

There were a small number of German prisoners billeted in the town. One dark night, on my way home, I found one of them sprawled on the pavement outside the door to his temporary home. I recognised him and thought he had been taken ill but such was not the case – he was intoxicated. I knocked on the door and was greeted by his landlady who I helped get him indoors. He was a tall, young, fair-haired handsome man, the sort you would associate with the 'Master Race'. Twenty years later, I was a member of the Territorial Army camping under canvas at Willsworthy. I was on sentry duty at the entrance to the site when a huge black Mercedes car drew up with a tall good-looking

The Congregational Church 1908. (Courtesy
Tavistock History Society)

fair-haired driver at the wheel, accompanied by his wife and two daughters. I knew him
at once as the former German prisoner I had helped but refrained from saying so, not
wishing to embarrass him. He wanted to drive onto the site and I would guess he was
about to show his family where he was first held prisoner all those years ago, but of course
I had to turn him away. He was a disappointed man but made no fuss and departed.

Somehow Mrs Martin made contact with two German officer POW's who were
permitted to visit her at her home (I think it may have been for the purpose of helping
maintain her large garden. Most prisoners were allocated to the farms). I was introduced
to them both and had no adverse feelings about doing so because they were so very
polite and interesting to talk to. One of them was a short plump man with piercing blue
eyes called Fritz; he was a jolly little chap who smoked a pipe with a huge bowl and a
curved stem. To my surprise he had been a Colonel in the German army. I asked him
once how he came to be captured and this is what he told me: 'I was in Normandy and
we knew the Allies had landed. We spent the night in a farmhouse and I told my men to
get some sleep because we would be very busy next day. At around two in the morning
we heard voices and someone shouting for us to come out with our hands up – we were
surrounded. It was a shock as we never thought the British could have advanced so
quickly. I said, "boys you had better do as he says because our position is hopeless" so
out we came and that was the end of my war', he laughed.

The second officer I only knew as Herr Lepichlau (not sure about the spelling), who was a tall, dark aristocratic-looking man who clicked his heels and kissed my mother's hand on the one occasion they met. My poor mother didn't know what to say or where to look. Both men stayed in the area after the war and were regular guests at Mrs Martin's house. They sent their hostess flowers on her birthday every year up until the time they did eventually go home. My father's reaction to all this was brief and to the point: 'What's wrong with having some of our boys to tea?' he asked and you couldn't argue with that. In his opinion it was practical Christianity that counted and he had many discussions with Mrs Martin on that issue. I well recall one Sunday evening returning from a walk with my parents and meeting my grandmother who had just attended evening service at the Abbey Chapel. The conversation revolved briefly around the virtue of going to worship on Sundays when my father remarked light-heartedly that half the ladies only went to see Mrs So-and So's new hat. My gran refuted this in no uncertain terms just as we approached the Congregational Church from which the congregation were emerging. A lady came straight over to us saying, 'Hello Mrs Doidge and have you seen Mrs. ____'s new hat?' My gran's face was a picture. My father had to look the other way.

By the time I was twelve, we had a little choir at the Abbey Chapel who sat in a separate pew below the pulpit and at a right angle to the worshippers. We performed songs arranged for us by our Minister. I do not believe anything like this had been done at the Abbey Chapel before and the kind words of approval we received afterwards from the congregation made it very worthwhile. Our musical group was comprised of: Trevor James (me), my sister Dilys, Glenda Roberts (my cousin), Angela Brooks, Christine Cornish, David Newnham and his younger brother Kenneth. David and I often sang solos and several times rendered 'Jerusalem' which was a favourite with our audience. The organist was Mr Reed, a talented pianist who lived next door to my family at Brooklands, assisted by Gerald Beaseley (?) who operated a wooden lever up and down behind the organ to pump the necessary air into it. We all took turns to do this job when for some reason Gerald wasn't available. An order of service was given to us to follow so that air was supplied at the right time for the several 'Amens' that were interspersed with the prayers (you cannot imagine the horrible squealing that occurred if you failed to do this). Mr Reed and Gerald were both employed at Tavistock Post Office.

The big event of the year was Harvest Festival which, although not on such a grand scale as the larger chapels and churches, was nevertheless fully supported. Every pew would be occupied and among the congregation would be representatives from Tavistock Hospital (usually Nurses), the Police, Fire Brigade, and of course a number of men and women from the other denominations in the town. Very often there would be guest soloists, my own father included, who I remember reciting Rudyard Kipling's 'Glory of the Garden'. One year we had the privilege of listening to a professional Negro singer, a Mr Rogers from Crownhill, who performed 'Swing Low Sweet Chariot' and some other spiritual songs in a rich bass voice that enthralled us. He was the first black man I ever saw in real life except for some American soldiers at a distance and he had a pleasant conversation with us youngsters when we were introduced to him afterwards.

Dear Mrs Martin was old-fashioned in every way, the image of the well-known 'Edwardian Lady' from her style of speaking, which was very 'correct' and never

The Abbey Chapel as it is today. (Author's photo)

included slang, to the way she dressed. Her clothing invariably was of a subdued colour, mainly light brown and ankle-length topped by a wide brimmed floppy hat. What an imposing figure she was, striding through Bedford Square, like a woman twenty years younger (she was a vegetarian and very slim). She was a widow and had no children of her own so I suppose we were substitutes in a way. Many a time she entertained us at her home in Courtenay Road for tea and perhaps a musical recital on her beautifully tuned harmonium (lots of Handel, my favourite composer, and perhaps a little Mozart). We played games like 'Here we come gathering nuts in May', long since out of vogue even then and slightly childish I thought; but she went to a lot of trouble and I suspect there were some sacrifices too (food rationing was still rigidly in force in 1946) to provide us with a lovely tea with cakes all of which were home-made. One Saturday in the summer she took us to Plymouth, and then by boat to Cawsand, where we were treated to ice creams and high tea, a generous gesture on her part and very much appreciated by us.

Mrs Martin eventually came to retirement and left Tavistock for her home town of Bury St. Edmunds, some time during the 1950s I think. I was abroad at the time so never had the opportunity to properly thank her for all she did for me and my family. She conducted the funeral services for my father and grandfather in the kindest way – if ever there were such a thing as a nice funeral they were prime examples. Her work as a Minister was carried out with dedication and concern for her parishioners; it included visiting them at home and a once a week (Friday) meeting with wives and grandmothers for tea and a chat, as well as a Sunday school session each Sabbath. For everything she ever did for us may I conclude this chapter by saying a fervent 'Thank You' to her for giving me so much loving attention all those years ago.

Did it all do me any good? you may ask. My answer is yes; of course it did. I have roamed the world since those days, and have been a sinner as most of us have but I truly believe I would have been a greater sinner without the benefit of those happy days in Sunday school and attending chapel later, not forgetting those wonderful people who taught me so much and whose respect I will forever hold dear.

Congregational Church Names

The occasion was the Church Anniversary 1943 and the picture was taken by two American soldiers. Image and names supplied by my cousin, the late Mrs Glenda Harvey (*nee* Roberts).

Front row L to R: Unknown, Hazel Maddock, Joyce Friend, Mary Evans, Jean Humphries, Glenda Roberts, Angela Brooks, Unknown, Dorthy Knott. Middle row (next to pillar) last two boys L to R: Roger Doidge, Trevor James (wearing cap)

Boyhood Days (Part 1)

My mother was born at Westbridge Cottages, and always said with pride she was born on one side of the river and Sir Francis Drake on the other (at Crowndale). Every true Tavistokian is proud of Sir Francis, mainly I think, because he rose from a humble birth to riches and fame as a result of his own endeavours. From an early age, I was regaled with tales of his exploits and often my parent's Sunday afternoon walks took us past Crowndale Farm where the great seafarer was born. Little trace now remains of the cottage his family occupied, but on the wall of the present day farmhouse there is a plaque to commemorate that event. I remember as a small boy going to Crowndale, accompanied by a friend with the specific object of examining the plaque, which had only recently come to our attention. With a sad lack of good manners we did not trouble ourselves with asking the occupants for permission, but climbed over the wall adjacent to the road and picked our way through the orchard. Before we reached our objective however, there was a shout from an enraged occupant waving a huge stick as he chased us off his property and cynically refused to believe our explanation that we only wanted to see where Drake was born (the apple trees were laden with fruit). I have since learned he was the maternal grandfather of Mr Toop the current owner and was universally known simply as 'Dolph', his full name being Randolph. My only recollection of him is a glimpse of an elderly gentleman wearing a brown trilby hat and brandishing the aforementioned stick after which I had my back towards him!

Like my mother I am proud to have been born in Drake's home town and have many happy memories which may be of interest to the reader. I was born on the first of October 1934 at No. 38 Brook Street where Somerfield's car park entrance now is. It was my grandparent's home where my mother and father first lived after they were married (my father was then a Leading Signalman in the Royal Navy). As a result, my earliest memories are of my grandparents, Mr and Mrs Charlie Doidge, one of several branches of the Doidge families who lived in the Tavistock area at that time. In fact, Doidge is a name rarely found outside West Devon. My grandfather was the gardener for the Bedford Hotel gardens in Plymouth Road (now the site of Tavistock car park). Then the entire car park area was one huge garden, which my grandfather tended single-handed for more than thirty years. He grew everything. I recall seeing potatoes, all kinds of green vegetables, carrots, beetroot, lettuces, and of course tomatoes and cucumbers, in the big greenhouse in the middle of the garden which had a boiler underneath and a large iron water tank on the outside. All the water was taken from the Tavistock canal, which flowed along one side as it still does. The garden was divided into squares where the various products were grown with box hedging all round and neatly trimmed at all times to a height of about 2 ft. Besides the vegetables there were every kind of fruit, from raspberries and gooseberries to red and black currants, strawberries, apples and

Statue of Sir Francis Drake, Plymouth Road, Tavistock. (Author's photo)

pears. On either side of the path which runs from the Plymouth Road entrance to the little bridge that spans the canal, there were apple and pear trees growing on the walls and polyanthus at their foot all the way along. Weeds were not permitted.

My grandfather had no mechanical aids which meant the entire garden was dug by hand – how he did it I will never know but he worked until he was seventy years of age when he handed over to a younger man who had another man to help him. I don't think he earned more than £3 a week in his life but never was there a more conscientious employee. I remember him taking me, from the age of three or four, to the garden on Sunday mornings when he would check all was well, pausing to adjust the greenhouse windows depending on the weather or, in the winter months, going down some steps to the tiny boiler underneath the greenhouse and topping up the furnace with coke. A gentleman called White owned the Bedford Hotel at that time and as a mark of appreciation for services faithfully rendered he gave his gardener £1 per week out of his own pocket when he retired. Not long afterwards, Mr White died and my grandfather lost his £1 a week. He never complained or bemoaned his lot; indeed my grandparents were the most contented couple I have ever known.

Most of their grocery items were delivered every week by a man called Dingley (I think). He worked for Mr Muzzlewhite whose grocery store was just a few yards away in Brook Street. Mr Muzzlewhite was a typical Victorian with grey hair and moustache and spectacles. He was a kindly man who knew all his customers by name, including family members, as did most tradesmen in those days. Dingley was a slim, middle-aged man, who rode an old fashioned delivery bike with thick tyres and an iron frame, with a small front wheel above which was an iron basket holder. Once a week he would appear wearing a brown dustcoat with a small cardboard box of provisions tied with string and a pencil

Brook Street as it used to be, and little has changed today. (Courtesy Tavistock History Society)

tucked behind one ear. 'Hello Mr Somebody' my grandmother would say (all tradesmen were 'Mr Somebody' to my gran) and in he would come for a cuppa and a chat. Then out of his pocket would come a battered notebook, and the pencil would be licked and poised before the enquiry 'Now Mrs Doidge?' Gran would give him her order for the following week but more often than not there would be an item she couldn't remember. Then Mr Dingley would take a deep breath and reel off practically every item sold in the shop with machine gun rapidity interrupted at an appropriate moment by 'Yes! That's what I forgot Mister Somebody – self-raising flour' (or some other necessity).

My grandmother was a wonderful cook who, in her young days, left home and became a cook for a Bishop in London. Later on she cooked for the Duke of Bedford at 'Endsleigh', his county estate, which is where she met my grandfather who was a gardener there. How often I have watched her peeling potatoes or apples at a speed you could scarcely credit. The item to be skinned revolved in her hand like a top and the knife sliced through the skin and deposited it in one circular piece. My grandfather always came home to lunch and sat to the table at 12 o'clock sharp when his meal would be put in front of him (I have seen my Gran run up Brook Street in a panic because 'Dad' would be home soon for his dinner and nothing had yet been prepared). From which you will gather they lived by the clock. I have often seen them sat in their living room on Fridays (market day) when my Gran would be sat knitting with her hat and coat on and my grandfather, with his raincoat on and hat and walking stick to hand, reading a cowboy book. He never read anything else and the little subscription library in King Street, of which he was a member, always put new 'Westerns' on one side for him because more often than not, over a period of many years, he discovered before he was halfway through a book that he had read it before. Every few minutes my Gran would look at the clock and when it was mid-day she would say 'well, old man'. Then he too would check the time and reply 'yes old woman' and they would get up and set off for the Pannier Market. They never called each other anything else except when my gran was displeased when she would address him as 'Charlie' which was his one and only name (or so we thought – see 'Introduction to my Family').

I well remember my gran putting me to bed in a tiny bedroom in their home in Brook Street with a small square window that looked to the sky. It was a feather bed and the most comfortable one I ever slept in. On a bedside table was a brass candlestick with a candle lighting the room with a warm glow. I was tucked up and given a picture book to look at, an old fashioned sort designed to encourage young readers to learn the alphabet. Each page had a huge coloured picture with the appropriate letter in black capitals beside it. Example: **A** is for **Apple** so rosy and red (how longingly I gazed at the juicy looking red apple portrayed) and further on: **C** is for **Candle** to light you to bed. I was too young to understand a word of it but do not recall ever getting beyond **C** before my eyes drooped and gran would appear to blow out the candle and ensure all was well.

Talking of red apples reminds me of my grandfather sitting in his favourite armchair with his back to the window where he could relax and read his newspaper. To his right was a dark wood 'dresser' with drawers. The top drawer always held some apples, deep red in colour, and of a particularly juicy kind. When visiting them grandpa would open that drawer on our departure with the words 'here you are – before you go' and hand over a choice sample from his little store. On occasion he would say nothing until we reached the front door on our way out by which time I and my sister Dilys would be in a panic thinking he'd forgotten (treats of any kind were rare during the war years) but then would come the call 'just a minute!' and back in we would go to receive our special gift and a smile from that dear old man who never really forgot.

Gran was a forthright woman who was never afraid to speak her mind. One day my grandfather fell very ill and the doctor had to be called. It was Dr Gillies and he diagnosed a fever and gave my grandmother a prescription with the words 'give him a dose of this twice a day and by next week he'll be much better. I'll call again then just to make sure'. The week went by and the doctor came once more as promised to find my grandfather out of bed and seemingly fully recovered. 'There you are – I told you that medicine I prescribed would do the trick' he declared. 'Medicine indeed!' said my grandmother. 'If you really want to know it didn't do him any good at all. I went down the lane and picked a few -------s (something wild and potent that I cannot remember the name of) and boiled it in a saucepan. He got better in no time after drinking that – never mind your medicine!' When she was employed at 'Endsleigh' the drive was close to where she lived with other women servants and when the Duke passed they were expected to line up outside and curtsey to the coach. My gran would never comply with this and stayed indoors with the curtains drawn until he'd gone by.

When I was still a small boy my parents went to live in Sunshine Terrace in Parkwood Road. My close friends were the Medland twins, John and David, who were orphans being cared for by their uncle and aunt whose surnames I cannot recall. I only know the boys were loved and cared for by them as if they were their own sons. We had some great times, culminating one day in me being buried up to my neck by them in a sandpit at their end of the terrace. My mother couldn't find me and was frantic with worry. That was a typical prank. On another occasion after a rainy morning we played making mud pies and

View of Brooklands House (centre left) surrounded by semi-detached dwellings all of which formed the Brooklands Estate. (Author's photo)

threw them at the 'Sunshine Terrace' sign mounted half way up the end wall which formed part of the house they lived in. We completely obliterated the sign and much of the wall, to the ensuing wrath of their aunt. John and David were identical twins in every respect and all my boyhood I could never tell them apart; this lasted into our teens when I had always to ask on meeting one of them 'are you John or David?' As it happened, one of them (I think it was John!) went to the Grammar School and his brother attended Dolvin Road, so in term time one could identify them by their clothing.

It must have been in 1938 when we moved to Brooklands House on the little housing development called simply 'Brooklands'. My mother remembered when Brooklands was a small estate owned by a General Jacobs (she also witnessed his funeral when she was a small child and saw his cortege on its way to the Unitarian Abbey Chapel as it then was). It was a lovely old house dating from 1803 and our flat (number one) was on the ground floor. There were five flats altogether. Next door to us at No. 2 lived Mr and Mrs Reed. Mr Reed held a good position in Tavistock Post Office and joined the Home Guard when war broke out. Whenever he passed our house in his uniform I always wanted to know when he was going to get a rifle; when he eventually was issued with one he stopped outside our front window and with a grin held it up for me to see. The upper flats were occupied by an Irish widow, Mrs Bartlett, Mr and Mrs Dunne, whose daughter Elsie was in the W.R.N.S. and their son Paddy; then there was Mrs Giles with her son Eric who was a great friend and playmate, the same age as me.

I believe our flat was the largest. There were two huge bedrooms, both with two sets of double French windows with wooden shutters and metal bars to secure them. The ceilings had decorated circular plasterwork which once surrounded chandeliers. All the doorways were about two foot in depth with solid mahogany doors and surrounds; the doors had big round white ceramic handles which required both my hands to turn them. Outside there was an iron frame, up which climbed an ancient Wisteria that produced enormous blooms each spring. This lovely plant curled upwards over the top of the frame and up the walls, turning a corner to a recess and pursuing its way almost up to roof level. It was a spectacular sight. Our front room used to be the library and was panelled in oak half way up the walls with a lovely bay window overlooking Parkwood Road and across the valley to Mount Tavy and the old Great Western railway line, the single track line from Plymouth to Launceston. The trains from Tavistock to Launceston emerged from a cutting and over a bridge across Mount Tavy Road, before traversing an embankment which we could clearly see. An indication of how the railways used to run lies in the remark my mother made nearly every morning: 'There's the ten past eight train! Hurry up and get ready (for school) and check the clock!'

At the rear of Brooklands was another embankment with a double track – the main Southern Railway line from Plymouth to Waterloo station in London. We always knew when the 'down' train was coming, because the doors and windows used to gently rattle followed by an actual ground-shaking tremble as it roared into view on its approach to Tavistock North station. My bedroom faced the railway and around 11 p.m. every night the clanking and clatter of metal could be heard as a late night goods train was being assembled in the extensive sidings; then came the deep 'chuffing' and rapid churning of the engine, as the wheels slipped, taking the strain and getting the train moving. Then the engine came into view, puffing smoke and sparks on the uphill gradient, with the driver's face clearly visible in the reflected glow of the firebox, followed by a line of goods trucks, and lastly the guards van with a red rear light. And this was all timed to the minute.

Our bathroom was a dismal place, with a huge frosted window looking out to the walled-in rear of the house, always cold and uninviting. On bath nights my mother had to fill a round free-standing metal boiler (referred to as a 'copper' but which in fact was aluminium) with a gas ring beneath to heat it and when the water was hot she baled it out into the bath. There was only cold water available in the taps and central heating was unheard of. Our front room and the two bedrooms had coal fireplaces; the bedroom ones were massive Georgian types with white Italian marble surrounds and mantelpieces. In fact, because of the rationing of fuel, only our front room fire was ever lit. The kitchen was a narrow rectangular shape, with a tiny window and sink at one end, and was eternally gloomy even when the gas lamp was lit, often in daytime. How my poor mother managed I will never know. Adjacent to the sink was the kitchen door leading to a tiny courtyard with entrances to a huge coalhouse and steps leading down to an underground cellar, all constructed of stone and green with age. My father had a go at growing mushrooms in the cellar, but for some reason the yield was not worth the effort. My sister Dilys recalls an incident when I lured her into the gloomy depths of the cellar and ran out to slam the door shut, leaving her a terrified prisoner screaming pitifully to be let out. That was during our father's absence of course, and had he been there I would undoubtedly have got the full retribution I deserved for such a callous act.

The house was a cold draughty place in winter and with the wartime rationing of fuel previously mentioned little comfort was to be had until we snuggled down in our beds at night. When my sister Dilys and I were small we were bathed in turn on 'bath night' in our front room in a large tin bath and if we were well behaved a treat was in store: we were each given a slice of bread and took it in turns to toast it over the glowing fire coals attached to a toasting fork which had two large prongs and a long handle. There were times when the toast fell into the fire and had to be retrieved and the surplus charcoal scraped away. Needles to say, with the rationing of bread, nothing was wasted and we ate it just the same with no ill effects! Our mother would then read us a story before tucking us up in bed, each with a stone hot water bottle, the likes of which are antiques today. I remember more than one winter when the toilet water froze and there was ice on the inside of our bedroom windows; the same was true of many older properties in the town then.

We did not have electricity and every room was lit by gas, our wireless being battery powered. All wirelesses in those days had what was called an 'accumulator' whose purpose I never discovered but which had to be taken for re-charging most weeks. One of my Saturday chores was to carry it to Messrs. Burch whose radio shop was in Brook Street (it extended into the archway that used to run at the side of the 'Tavistock Hotel') and go back at the end of the day to collect it. My grandparents economised by listening only to the news and 'Sunday Half Hour' which as the name implies was a half hour programme of hymn singing broadcast live from various churches around the country.

Throughout the war, people everywhere discussed how much longer it would go on and often made wild predictions based on the latest news from the battlefields. My sister and I wanted our father home but to our shame rarely mentioned that fact to our mother, but when we did ask her reply was more often than not 'when the war is over I suppose'. Half the time, like every family who had relatives serving in the armed forces, we did not know where he was. His last posting was to Malta, and lasted from 23rd October 1943 to 31st March 1845, during which time he was with the Eighth Army in Sicily and Italy.

Tucked away in a cupboard at our home was the largest Union Jack you ever saw. It was well-worn and I used to think it came from a battleship which it probably did (my father was in Signals). I used to ask to see it and sometimes it was unravelled for us. 'We'll hang that one outside when the war ends' my mother used to say and when asked how we would know when the war was over the answer always was 'when you hear the church bells ring again you'll know' (that I believe was what happened when the First World War ended). When the war did finally end we did hang that flag outside. It was on VE Day, and like people all over Britain there was a tea party for us children and it was held outside our front window on level ground where there was room for the several tables laid end to end. Our Union Jack hung outside just as my mother promised, over the wall above the wool factory, where it could be seen by passers-by in Parkwood Road. Then it rained, not heavily, but sufficient for us to seek shelter and ended with the tables and chairs and all the children at Brooklands having their celebration tea in my bedroom (a large room previously described).

Later that year, there was a Victory Parade in Tavistock. I remember it was raining but the streets were crowded nonetheless to see the band of the Royal Marines leading contingents of sailors, Royal Marines in No. 1 uniforms, Marines with muskets dressed in uniforms of

Nelson's day and a number of 'boy sailors' (all of them sons of serving or deceased naval fathers and average age eleven or twelve I should think) pulling two undersized field guns. Despite the rain all of them were the smartest body of men (and boys) you ever saw. The sailor boys then gave a display in Bedford Square which resembled the famous field gun competitions the Royal Navy was renowned for. Afterwards I observed the participants seated in the back of the 'ten ton' lorries that took them back to Plymouth, all of them soaking wet and singing at the top of their voices. I remarked about this to my father with some astonishment and was told, 'That is the spirit of real men my son. Let nothing daunt you'. During my varied life since then I have found that advice to be very true.

Our landlord was Mr W. H. Gulley, who owned not only our house but the whole of Brooklands and numerous other properties in Tavistock. He was a prosperous self-made man of mature years and, it must be said, was an imposing figure with his shock of white hair, bushy white moustache, a wide girth beneath a pin-striped suit with a waistcoat to match, from which hung a silvery watch-chain in a curve. He owned the Model Laundry in Parkwood Road adjacent to Sunshine Terrace and had done for very many years. It was there my mother had her first job at fourteen years of age as a laundry assistant at the rate of one and a half pence per hour (old money). Mr Gulley for some reason was known to his employees as 'Blackbird' but commanded a lot of respect by taking off his jacket and joining in all kinds of work to be done when the need arose. My grandmother told me she could remember when he sold meat 'door to door' in Tavistock from a straw basket. He progressed to selling meat and poultry to outlying villages with the aid of a pony and trap. Later still, he opened a butcher shop in Yelverton before buying into the laundry where he made his fortune.

To continue, our landlord would appear at least once every year to inspect his property, not to snoop on us but to put right any defects. He always knocked on the door and

View of Duke Street from Bedford Square. (Courtesy of Tavistock History Society)

greeted my mother in a friendly manner. 'Hello Kath' he would say (her name was Kathleen) 'may I come in?' 'Yes of course', and taking off his hat he would enter asking if there was anything that needed attention. Most times my mother had nothing to tell him but he would spot something every time, maybe a crack in the plaster ceiling or a drip from a gutter, and say something like 'that won't do Kath – I'll send someone around to fix that in a day or two'. Sure enough, in a day or two a man would come and do repairs.

The rest of Brooklands comprised several semi-detached modern houses which are still there today, some having been enlarged. During those wartime years the following occupiers come to mind:

Next door lived Mr and Mrs Murray whom I was very wary of because they had no children (unless they were grown) and were strict about how you were expected to go about getting your ball back from their garden; for example, you had to knock on the door and ask politely. He worked at the wool factory below our house and was an energetic man who lived a quiet life together with his wife. Mr Murray was a keen gardener and their garden was always immaculate and a joy to behold, with pretty flowers everywhere and a separate vegetable plot. One morning there was a loud roar and a cloud of dust arose from the area below his vegetable garden (on one side of which was a sheer drop of about thirty feet) leaving a rugged crater where there had once been a beautifully tended plot. The retaining wall had given way and some cars parked beneath were crushed in a heap of soil and rubble. I saw Mr Murray come home for lunch as usual with barely a glance at the gap where his beloved garden had once been and he never said a word to anyone about it. When I met him and his wife years later during a spell of home leave from the Merchant Navy we had a most friendly and interesting conversation when I was amazed to hear about his experiences in the wilderness of Western Canada (my ship was on a regular run to Canada at that time). He was a quiet, modest man who lived a quiet and contented life, not at all the adventurous type he obviously had once been.

Next to them were Mr and Mrs Stevens, with their two daughters Christine and her elder sister June, who became a prefect at the Grammar School. Mr Stevens was a railwayman who worked at Tavistock South station, always referred to as the 'Great Western' station in those days. Next to the Stevens family lived an older couple, with their daughter Mrs Merritt, whose husband was a prisoner of war under the Japanese in Singapore. Then there was Mrs Bartlett and her young daughter Christine. I did not know it at the time but her husband was serving in North Africa with the Eighth Army. All the above mentioned families lived at an address called 'The Lawn' which of course stemmed from General Jacob's occupancy of the big house.

Then there were the people who lived in 'The Drive' which, as the name implies, was the uphill approach to the estate. The very first residence was at the junction of The Drive with Parkwood Road and was named 'The Lodge'. During the war years my best friend Trevor Saundry and his elder brother Barry lived there with their mother and grandfather. When I grew up and got engaged I learned from their father that he knew my future father-in-law, the late Mr E. J. Batten of Brentor; they had served together during the war in the Royal Engineers. Further up the hill, in the first house on the left, above the little bridge which crossed the leat that powered the

Trevor James aged eight.

Parkwood Road mill, lived Mr and Mrs Hodge and their two grown sons Cyril and ????
Mr Hodge was a Great Western Railway employee who worked with Mr Stevens. Next
to them were Mr and Mrs Lyons and their little daughter Christine. Mr Lyons was one
of the first men in Tavistock to go to war and I can see him now, striding along Brook
Street in army uniform carrying a kitbag on his shoulder, saying a cheerful goodbye to
everyone he knew. Not long afterwards he was back at home, minus a leg, after the lorry
he was in hit a mine in France.

The next house was the home of Mr and Mrs Potter and their son Terry and two
daughters Molly and Tracy. Mr Potter was a very smartly dressed man who usually wore
a grey suit and trilby hat. He worked in a bank. Sadly he died young, leaving his widow
to bring up their three children single-handed. Then there were Mr and Mrs Rich and their
two grown daughters Esmie and ???? Mrs Rich was very fond of dogs and her dog was
very well trained and obedient to every verbal command. The last house before rounding
the corner and entering 'The Nook' was occupied by several people whose relationship
I never got to know about. One was Mrs Gane, a very pleasant lady who was the ticket
cashier at the then relatively new Carlton Cinema situated at the junction of Russell Street
and Plymouth Road (demolished in 2005 and replaced by a hideous block of flats totally
out of character with Tavistock). My friend Angela Brooks was her daughter. Towards the
end of the war a Mr Truman lived there. He was a Royal Marine who saw much active
service and was idolised by me from afar whenever I saw him coming and going in his best
uniform. I loved the Royal Marines and it was my one ambition to join that illustrious
Corps, but it was not to be – my eyesight wasn't good enough when I applied.

The furthest group of houses comprised 'The Nook', situated up and behind
Brooklands House and there were nine pairs of semi-detached dwellings. Among the
residents were Mr and Mrs Lang, the parents of Mrs Dunne and grandparents of
their two children 'Paddy' and Marion. Next door to them were Mr and Mrs Crocker
who had a very pretty daughter with golden hair and big blue eyes called Dulcie; then
came the Maddock family. Mr Maddock was a big jovial man who was employed at
the slaughterhouse in Market Road and was also a part time fireman. His daughter
Hazel was in my class at 'Council School', and when I met her recently after more than
sixty years she was just the same pleasant and likeable person I remembered. She had
two younger brothers, Graham and Harry. Next door again were Mr and Mrs Spiller
whose daughter Jill attended the Grammar School. Mr and Mrs Littlejohns were their
neighbours, a quiet couple without any children. Mr Littlejohns was a tall, handsome
man who fought at Arnhem with the Parachute Regiment and was evacuated early on
with a serious leg wound that left him with a permanent limp. My mother, my two
younger sisters and I lived next to them after my father died.

Other families I recall living at The Nook were Mr and Mrs Stephens and their two
sons; Mr and Mrs Trethewey who had a young daughter; Mr and Mrs Cloak, and Mr
and Mrs Bond with their daughter Joyce and son Keith, both older than me. Mr Bond
was a quiet and thoroughly nice man; he was also a Plymouth Argyle fanatic who
supported them at matches all over the country.

This was the home background to my childhood days and I am sorry to say I and my
pals were the cause of much aggravation to some of the residents at Brooklands during
those war years, about to be described in Part Two.

Boyhood Days (Part 2)

I would not have changed my upbringing or experiences as a boy for anything. I think my young days were unusual in many ways and not because there was a war raging or that we were 'invaded' by hoards of American soldiers; neither was it because we were all forced to live frugally because of the rationing or the fact that so many of us had absent fathers serving in the armed forces. It was a combination of all these things: the excitement of the battles being fought and the bombing of nearby Plymouth. I often saw the red glow in the sky, the criss-crossed searchlights seeking the enemy planes as that city was blitzed during 1942. We saw the aftermath on our rare visits to that devastated city. We also witnessed the strange ways of the American soldiers with their distinctive easy-going drawl when they spoke. Then there was the relative freedom we enjoyed without fathers to exercise the essential discipline young lads need. Our harassed mothers were struggling to feed and clothe us on barely substantial rations, not to mention the worry about their husbands and the threat of invasion by the Germans.

For us boys though, it was a thrilling time and most of us ran wild over the town and countryside. Our favourite playground was the little wood opposite the row of cottages adjacent to Vigo Bridge in Mount Tavy Road. It consisted of a steep bank under the trees with a cliff to one side. On the summit you looked down on the Great Western railway line cutting through, which the trains en route to Launceston passed after leaving the G.W.R. station at Tavistock South and before crossing the black iron bridge that spanned the road. We (I and my friends the Saundry brothers, Trevor and his elder brother Barry) regularly trespassed on the line to lay penny coins on the rails and watch the trains run over them until they were pressed into elongated oval shapes which became curiosities to swap with other boys for marbles, etc. One day we ventured on to the bridge and became so engrossed in arranging our pennies we failed to notice the approach of the 'down' train until it was too late. Trevor and I were lucky enough to run to safety but his brother Barry was trapped halfway across the bridge. His only option was to lie flat between the rails and the side of the bridge, which was quite narrow, and he must have felt the heat from the engine as its huge churning wheels went by just inches from his face. It was a frightening experience which we took care not to repeat.

Most groups of boys called themselves a 'gang' and the gang I belonged to (only four in number) did everything together. We were greatly influenced by the films we saw every Saturday afternoon at one of Tavistock's two cinemas, the Carlton Cinema already mentioned and what we always referred to as the 'Old Cinema' (converted from the former Corn Exchange – these words can still be seen cut into the stone overhead) on the corner of West Street and King Street, where for fourpence we watched the 'big' film and the serial. There was always a second 'B' film but for our scanty offering we were

West Street with the 'Old Cinema' (right). (Courtesy Tavistock History Society)

turned out after the serial to make way for patrons who paid the full rate for the first of the two evening performances.

The serial I remember most vividly was called 'Overland Mail' and ran for over a year. It was about the pony express riders and the first stagecoaches traversing the plains of the 'Wild West'. The hero was Jim Lane (played by actor William Elliot) whose incredible adventures were played out by us afterwards. He always wore black and had two silver-coloured six guns worn in an unusual way with the butts facing forwards; his speciality was out-gunning his opponents with a 'cross draw' motion that never failed. Naturally nearly every boy I knew emulated this feat either with toy guns (in short supply during the war years) or with home-made imitations. Then there were the Errol Flynn masterpieces – The *Sea Hawk, Captain Blood, Charge of the Light Brigade* etc., every one of which fired our imaginations to the 'nth' degree. The greatest impression made on us however was Tyrone Power's leading role in 'The Black Swan', a saga of the Spanish Main where he took the part of a pirate captain nicknamed 'Jamie Boy'. Naturally in our re-enactments I was 'Jamie Boy' ever afterwards and such was the extent of our enthusiasm we manufactured wooden swords and wooden daggers to hold between clenched teeth. We fastened the top button only of the gabardine raincoats most of us wore at that time so that they were transformed into cloaks which in turn transformed us into swashbuckling adventurers.

Come to think of it, I had an armoury consisting of a wooden sword with a cocoa tin lid for a guard, a wooden home-made dagger, a war club made from a thick chunk of tree branch with individual patterns cut out of the bark and a dustbin lid shield. We each manufactured daggers from strips of softwood which we cut to shape with our pocket knives (every boy had one in those days) and then spent hours rubbing the blades with sandpaper until we had a perfectly smooth sharp-edged weapon any pirate would have been proud of. I remember sitting in the front row of the cinema with other like-minded boys all rasping away throughout the film, by which time the result of our labours were satisfactory. I sometimes wonder how it was we were never ejected what with the noise we made and the scattering of sawdust we left in our wake. Our array of weaponry was completed by the addition of a bow and arrows. We all knew where to go to find the best hedgerow for obtaining materials, when several fearsome weapons were manufactured and tested in competitions where we fired arrows the longest distance or into the air the highest. We graduated to arrows that would penetrate tree trunks by fixing darning needles or darts points to the ends. It was a miracle no-one was ever seriously hurt or blinded by these activities and I suppose today they would be outlawed. The fact remains no-one I knew or heard of was ever injured in our make-believe battles.

To continue my tale of escapades I should add how, on occasion, we would stalk our 'enemies' and fire arrows into their gardens with notes attached declaring 'war a three o'clock', for example, after which we would rush to our beloved wood and lay ambushes, dig pits and cover them with twigs and leaves for booby traps, stockpile odds and ends of wood or cabbage stumps to use as missiles when the enemy appeared. One day we discovered some empty oil drums and heaved them into position on the cliff top and toppled them over onto the foe. I feel sure these ideas stemmed from tales of warfare (some true, some of them fiction) in the films we saw or in the newspapers. We were commandos, fighter pilots, Seventh Cavalry 'dog soldiers', buccaneers; always fighting men of the highest calibre. Incidentally my younger sister Dilys was often enrolled as 'nurse' although she sometimes did her share of combat as well.

One day a group of us had engaged in a fierce battle with clubs and swords in Brooklands Drive just below the bridge over what was then a leat which supplied the nearby flour mill. Shouts and warlike cries rent the air as swords clattered on dustbin lids and stones flew from beneath scuffling feet (the drive did not have a tarmac surface at that time). The climax came when a shrill voice was heard above the noise of combat: 'Oh my! Oh my! At this rate we won't be able to get to our own homes soon!' It was a lady resident with her basket of shopping and I am pleased to report the fighting stopped at once, the ranks divided and the good lady passed unscathed but the moment she was safely on her way battle began again with renewed vigour. I am afraid we sometimes gave our neighbours a hard time.

We set impossible tasks for boys who might want to join our gang (no-one ever did as membership was by invitation only and restricted to those who lived near to us). 'Recruits' would have had to jump from impossible heights, climb un-climbable trees, perform outstanding swimming feats, all of which none of us could have undertaken – with one exception: walking upright along the parapet of Vigo Bridge. I myself walked some distance it along on one occasion watched with horror by my grandmother, whose front room in Brook Street had a clear view of the bridge. It was a talking point in our

The view from the parapet of Vigo Bridge unchanged today except for the church steeple. (Courtesy Tavistock History Society)

family for weeks afterwards, accompanied by dire warnings about the dangers and how lucky I was not to have fallen. I wasn't punished but was left in no doubt that, far from being the hero I aspired to become when I did it, the reality was it was a foolish prank which would bring retribution on a grand scale if I ever did such a thing again.

On quiet days we would go fishing – catching 'tiddlers' in the Tavistock canal. They were actually called Minnows and were caught in jam-jars attached to a length of string. We lay for hours on our bellies on the tennis court side of the canal, peering into the water waiting for our intended victims to enter our jars which faced downstream. Sooner or later one was sure to make that mistake when we would instantly yank our jar to the surface with the tiny fish swimming in circles within. Sometimes we put them into a spare jar we brought for the purpose and 'fished' for more. On other occasions we inserted a crumb or two of bread into our glass traps as an inducement and carefully lowered away; it never failed to attract the little creatures. When we tired of this activity we put our catches back into the canal having learned it was a mistake to take them home as, after perhaps only a day, we would find them floating belly up quite dead. We were quite ignorant of the fact they probably died after using up all the oxygen in the small amount of water they lived in.

Then there was a trolley craze. Nearly all my friends manufactured a trolley from planks of wood and discarded pram or pushchair wheels, most of which had a seat in the form of a wooden fruit box nailed to the frame and ropes attached to the outer ends of the front axle to steer with. Some of us disdained to use ropes and steered with our feet. We hurtled down hills with reckless delight without brakes (your booted heels did the trick if you really needed it) and a danger to anyone unfortunate enough to get in

The Meadows and Tavistock Canal. We caught 'minnows' from the grassy bank (left). (Courtesy Tavistock History Society)

our way, including other road users. All the same no-one to my knowledge was killed or badly hurt, although we all bore the scars and bruises as a result of colliding with walls or simply overturning at speed. It was a common sight in Tavistock at one time to see trolleys being towed through the streets on some mission or other. I once pulled mine all the way to Walreddon Manor to 'scrump' (steal) apples. Together with a friend who lived at Rix Hill we filled our box seats to the brim with a mixture of cookers and eaters, telling our mothers the most outrageous tales as to how we got them. We couldn't very well take them back so they were made good use of and very nice too were the pies and tarts produced.

More often than not the baked products of the apples we brought home were enhanced by the addition of blackberries we picked. Our favourite spot for this activity were the quarry workings at Wilminstone which was, at that time, in full production but deserted at weekends. It seemed everyone we knew were gathering the huge juicy berries that dangled from overhanging precipices, ignoring the dangers in their determination to obtain the best of the harvest. Our mothers would have had heart attacks if they'd seen us – or would they? I often think they must have got up to the very same pranks as children which was how they knew to tell us where and where not to go.

My friends the Saundry brothers returned to Plymouth to live when their father came home from wartime service in the Army. I saw them at their Plymouth home from time to time, and on one occasion was appalled when they showed me the metal knuckle-dusters they always carried. 'You have to be prepared to look after yourself down here' I was told but I think it was mostly bravado because they were decent lads from a respectable family. In any case, after all the escapades we shared not once did any of us display the slightest malicious or aggressive behaviour except on one particular occasion.

One day, four of us fell out over cigarettes (yes, we were old hands at smoking at eight or nine years of age). The Saundry brothers, me and another boy called Keith Bond (sadly now deceased) used to pool our paltry pocket money and take it in turns to buy packets of five Woodbines for the Saundry's grandfather (who only ever smoked a pipe). There were no restrictions then about selling tobacco products to children who, more often than not, were genuinely on an errand for their parents. I well remember the smallest packets of fags being sold in paper packets of five which was all we could afford. Usually we tossed a coin for the privilege of having the odd cigarette after the contents were shared between the four of us but on this occasion Keith, who had contributed the most, felt it should be his to have. All this took place in the Saundry household coal house at the rear of The Lodge at the bottom of Brooklands Drive. It caused a bitter argument which culminated in Keith storming off up the hill with the intention of telling my mother where I was and that I was smoking. As it happened, my mother was not at home, but in his absence his own mother passed by and we were delighted to inform her of what Keith had been doing just as he reappeared. Needless to say he 'caught it' good and proper after which we three survivors enjoyed the spoils out of sight in the coalhouse gloom. My mother found out of course, and this incident was just one too many on top of all my other misdeeds. 'I'm going to tell your father about this' I was told, and 'he'll deal with you when he comes home my lad' (father was away in the war). Well, he came home at last and every mealtime I would study his face wondering if my mother had told him yet and what dire fate would be mine. It never happened and the only comment he ever made was in a letter my mother once showed me where he stated 'So Trevor has been smoking – well of all the things I did as a boy I never smoked'.

All the above occurred up to the age of eleven after which I and many of my friends separated, some to attend the Grammar School, others to be enrolled at Dolvin Road. The boys I knew were my friends for life – it was just that we all made new acquaintances and developed fresh interests. Most of us had bicycles by this time and at weekends and holidays we made good use of them exploring the surrounding area. We cycled to Brentor and West Down, among other places, racing one another down the hills without a thought for our safety or anyone else's. In the summer months our destinations included Denham Bridge where we dived and swam in the rocky gorge beneath. Someone had rigged a thick rope to an overhanging tree which we took turns to grab hold of and swing out over the river, letting go at the highest point and dropping vertically into the water to try and touch the bottom. No-one ever did and little wonder: I discovered in later life the 'gorge' was formed by the tin miners blasting their way through, in their efforts to mine the precious metal and that the depth was (and is) more than forty foot. By the way, once you did your 'Tarzan' act with the rope there was no coming back – your pals wouldn't let you so you were committed to the drop. Many trips were made to the 'Moorland Links Hotel' on Roborough Down who charged sixpence for unlimited use of their swimming pool. The attraction? It had a slide.

Tavistock Carnival was initiated shortly after the end of the war when I was on the point of leaving my home town to go to sea. Key figures in this project included Mr S. Goode, landlord of the 'White Hart', Mr E. Whitaker, Editor of the *Tavistock Times*,

May Revels. May Queen Audrey Weekes with Attendants Peggy Bowhay (left) and another unknown. (Courtesy Tavistock History Society)

and Mr Richards, a Western National Bus Company Inspector. It was a success from the start and is still going strong today.

One of the highlights every year was the May Revels performed by Dolvin Road School. There was always a May Queen to be chosen together with Attendants and they formed the pinnacle of the day's events. The picture of May Queen Audrey Weeks dates from 1948. Succeeding Queens included Peggy Bowhay, Pamela Youlden and Betty McNicoll. The whole school participated and practised for weeks beforehand the various entertainments they performed. There was a Maypole with coloured ribbons allocated to the youngest pupils who danced the traditional Maypole Dance on the vicarage lawn to music and the delight of the spectators. Some years there was a Floral Dance through the town via Vigo Bridge, Brook Street, Duke Street, Bedford Square and so to the Vicarage, where the children performed country dancing, displays, and singing. Each event was introduced by my wife June James (*nee* Batten) when she was Head Girl in 1949, her final year. For the Floral Dance it was often necessary for some of the girls to dress as boys because not every boy would want to take part in that particular event. My sister Dilys once had that chore and wore stockings over long breeches and a tailed coat. She didn't mind – it was all good fun. Another time she joined her friends in dancing 'Gavotte' style. This dance dates from the time of King Louis XIV of France, and was originally a popular country dance in Brittany. They were thrilled to dress up in the style of the French Court in full length dresses with long sleeves with frilled lace cuffs and a 'ruff' around their necks, not forgetting a large 'beauty spot' painted on one cheek! Powdered wigs and a wide brimmed floppy hat completed their outfits, all very colourful and exciting for young girls. One year, the boys paraded through the town dressed in 'Lincoln Green' and carrying bows and arrows and wooden swords as members of Robin Hood's 'Merry Men'. Their performance at the Vicarage included a 'sword dance' during which, after much clattering of wooden blades and complicated manoeuvring, ended with a huge star-shaped emblem consisting entirely of interlocked 'swords' being held aloft. Another time they gave a magnificent gymnastic display identical to that performed by the R.A.F. at tournaments etc. They were trained by Mr Hopkins, their Geography teacher, who had been a pilot in the R.A.F. during the Second World War. When the Grammar School and Dolvin Road School merged to become Tavistock Comprehensive School in later years, all such celebrations terminated and I believe the town is poorer for that.

Tavistock swimming pool has been described in part one of my schooldays and was very well patronised on Saturday afternoons when every boy and girl in Tavistock, it seemed, queued for admission at 2 p.m. and paid twopence (it may have been fourpence) admission charge before racing for the changing rooms in an attempt to be first in the pool. We boys wore our trunks instead of underpants to speed up the process and I do not recall a girl ever jumping in ahead of us. There was a two level diving board and a springboard. The champion diver and a reckless jumper from the top board was a small boy known as 'Tacker', but whose name I cannot remember. Tacker lived at the top of Bannawell Street only a door or two away from the Prouse brothers who were older lads. All three were magnificent swimmers and one of the brothers often performed his favourite 'party trick' for us by lighting a cigarette and putting it in his mouth with the lighted end inside. He then swam the length of the pool under water and took a puff from the still-lit fag to cheers from us all.

For most of us a trip to the swimming pool was a treat but there were not so many fourpences forthcoming for more regular attendances so an alternative venue was used on all other days. The River Tavy flows under Mount House School and past Kelly College after cascading over a weir hidden from the road by a stone wall. It was known as 'Evan's Weir' and I have often thought it must have been named after the Rev. Evans, a Unitarian Minister whose daughter Rachel was the well-known Dartmoor writer. They lived in the large house opposite the stone wall and whose entrance was by the little bridge where a leat flows towards the town. Years later it became the residence for the Headmaster of Kelly College. The weir was the place many of us youngsters, all in our teens, met most evenings from May to September. Access was through a gap in the hedge at the Tavistock end of the wall and along the GWR railway track which ran alongside the road at this point. We then crossed a corner of a field that belonged to the farm which at that time occupied the space opposite College Avenue where there is now a small housing development. The farm was on the other side of the railway embankment which once was there. We never took any other liberties on the farmland (now playing grounds for Kelly College) and there was no vandalism of any kind which is probably why we were never apprehended.

There was a deep pool under the weir itself with convenient rocks from which to dive into the cold clear waters. I have been swimming there after heavy rain when the water was a muddy brown in colour, foaming and icy cold. I also remember an occasion when there was a thunderstorm and the river rose in minutes to a fast flowing torrent. It did not deter us from having our dip, which on reflection was a foolhardy thing to do. The girls crossed over to the other side to change (during the summer the river level was

Evans' Weir, Parkwood Road, Tavistock as it is today. (Author's photo)

usually low and it was easy to paddle to across the edge of the weir) whilst the boys sheltered on the Parkwood Road side to change and dry themselves afterwards. There was no familiarity of any kind except on one occasion when a certain boy upset the others and was forcibly divested of his trunks whilst in the water. The natural shyness that prevailed in those days meant he couldn't come out until the girls left and they were in no hurry to do so. At last the shivering victim gave a shouted warning he was coming out regardless – and he did just that whilst the girls' simpering smirks turned to screams of alarm as they fled back over to their side of the River Tavy.

One Saturday afternoon three or four of us decided to walk back home along the railway track. We were on the embankment referred to previously, chatting and laughing, when I heard a hissing sound and turned to see the engine of a passenger train almost upon us – literally. The train was silently coasting along the downhill gradient to Tavistock. A warning yell triggered a panic leap out of the way and us tumbling down the steep bank to safety. We were trespassing of course, in a reckless manner, and I have a vivid memory of the fright it gave me and my friends. We never again did such a thing, but I have wondered since what on earth the engine driver was doing not to have seen us and how he would have fared had a fatality occurred with an inquest to answer to.

The Yanks Are Coming!

I cannot recall the year but I must have been eight or nine years old when my mother and I met my Aunt Jane in Brook Street, Tavistock. 'Have you heard the news?' asked my aunt. 'What news is that?' said my mother. 'The Yanks are coming!' There was a pause, then 'Thank God! Now we'll show them!' ('Them' were the Germans).

For the record, the first American troops arrived in Britain in January 1942 only seven weeks after the Japanese attack on Pearl Harbour. The first American soldiers came to Tavistock in June 1943.

I think my mother's sentiments were widely shared. The battle at El Alamein had been won and the Red Army were driving the Germans back from Stalingrad, but how much longer could Britain and Russia keep up the pressure? There can be no doubt the seemingly unlimited manpower and huge input of armaments from the United States ensured ultimate victory from the moment they entered the conflict.

Tavistock then was not the bustling commercial place it is today. Before the war began it was a quiet market town that only came to life on Fridays (market day) and the annual Goose Fair day. Apart from members of the Armed Forces, few Tavistokians had travelled to foreign parts and America was as far away, figuratively speaking, as the moon. Our only conception of that great country arose from the cowboy films, musicals and romantic Hollywood stories based on characters who lived in affluent houses or lavish apartments.

Then they were here. The 29th U.S. Infantry Division, commanded by Major General Charles H. Gerhardt, was the first arrival and set up camp in June 1943 on Whitchurch Down with their headquarters at Abbotsfield House (now Abbotsfield Hall Nursing Home) in Tavistock. They were a part of V Corps, United States 1st Army under Lt. General Omar N. Bradley and were earmarked for the invasion of Europe. The residents of the town looked with a mixture of curiosity and some surprise at the sight of very smartly dressed young men in immaculately tailored uniforms and funny hats strolling among them chewing gum, talking with their distinctive drawl and eyeing the girls with equal interest.

A month later, more than 500 U.S. Army medical personnel, including 120 officers and nurses, arrived to take over the British-built camp at Plaster Down and established the 115th Field Hospital. It was to serve the needs of all U.S. Army, U.S. Navy and Coastguard bases in and around the Plymouth area. Most of the staff had experience working in civilian hospitals and were well able to deal with any type of patient they received. The unit had undergone intensive military training at Camp Shanks in New York State to enable them to be self sufficient in guarding, managing, maintaining and repairing their premises in addition to their main task of caring for the sick and

Abbotsfield Nursing Home, formerly Abbotsfield House, as it is today. (Author's photo)

wounded. The hospital was equipped with a laboratory and dental facilities as well as 750 beds (increased later to 1,480 in anticipation of invasion casualties) for all manner of wounded men.

As the build up of forces prior to D-Day continued into 1944 the roads and commons over a wide area around Plymouth and Tavistock filled with tented camps and vehicles of all kinds. Everything they needed, from clothing and food, to tobacco and Coca-cola, was imported from the U.S. Except water, of course. At Brentor there was a village 'chute' which comprised a miniature waterfall at the side of the road (it is still there) that provided pure drinking water from a spring and was at that time the main source of water for many residents. It became a meeting place for soldiers and a number of villagers, especially children, when they came every day with 'jerry' cans to replenish their supplies.

All Americans love children and for these men, far from home, it was an opportunity to make friends and delight them with little gifts – chocolate perhaps, or packets of gum. Often they would tell them to be there the following day and be sure to tell their 'Moms' to let them have jars or tins which they filled with tea (as valuable as gold dust to the recipients) or sugar, items which were strictly rationed in wartime Britain. Lucky youngsters would sometimes get invited for high speed rides in a jeep whilst their comrades got the water. Christmas 1943 was a memorable one for children who lived in and around Plymouth and Tavistock. They were treated, with typical American generosity, to celebration parties with no holds barred in the presentation of gifts and sweets and food on a lavish scale compared to the austere wartime rationing allowances. The writer remembers them taking over one of the two cinemas in Tavistock for a day

Dr. 'Tom' Davey (left) with Captain Gardner U.S. Army in the grounds of Abbey House. (Courtesy of Tavistock History Society)

when every child was invited to a film show, the entrance 'fee' being an empty glass jar or some old newspapers for recycling towards the war effort. The children were welcomed with smiles and wisecracks as well as a numbered ticket for the raffle that took place half way through the show. A friend of mine won a brand new baseball bat but didn't know what to do with it afterwards, and I think it simply became a memorable relic with which to remember a happy event. We watched Walt Disney cartoons and a cowboy film, and on our way out there were the army boys with huge kitbags from which they took large packets of 'candies' for every one of us.

Soldiers, sailors and airmen of many nationalities appeared in Tavistock from time to time but the Americans outnumbered them and seemed to be everywhere at all times. They played baseball in the meadows and there was a social club for them in West Street. In Duke Street there used to be a large garage ('Matthews Garage') where a lot of repair work was done to U.S. Army vehicles by their own mechanics. We boys used to congregate at the rear of the garage in Market Road and watch them. A favourite ploy was to ask the nearest one, 'are you a cowboy mister?' Often he was not but on occasion he would call out 'Hi Tex! These guys want to meet a cowboy' and tall lanky 'Tex' would come out smiling to be viewed by us with wonderment and some disappointment at his headgear – the inevitable baseball type cap with the peak turned up in jaunty manner.

They attracted the girls too. The best seats in the cinemas were occupied by them and their young lady friends, the sight of which caused envy among the uniformed British as well as some local lads. Sad to say a section of the community looked down on young women who went out with 'the Yanks', which was unkind to say the least, as the vast majority of them were disciplined, courteous and well behaved. I do not think there was ever any serious trouble in the town except a few scuffles between the white soldiers and some black ones. The Military Police patrolled the town wearing their distinctive white helmets – we called them 'Snowdrops' – and any soldier found misbehaving was quickly taken into custody and whisked back to camp.

During the war years the town was in complete darkness under the 'blackout' regulations and the meadows acquired an unsavoury reputation because of the 'goings on' that took place at night. It was all too true and traces of the 'goings on' were to be seen next day in the shelters and other secluded spots (I leave a full description to your imagination). The same things occurred in Crowndale Woods, to the shock and dismay of some prim and proper inhabitants, who blamed the American soldiers who, in truth, were almost certainly the main offenders. They could have been more discreet in their activities, but it should be remembered these were young men who did not know if they were going to survive the war and wanted to experience a loving affair before marching into battle. As a matter of fact, most of them did die on the beaches of Normandy and we owe them a debt we can never repay.

The Visiting Forces Act of 1942 allowed American Military Justice to be enacted on British soil. The Act provided for capital punishment and not only for murder; rape was also a capital offence in their army. Some soldiers were sent back to America to be executed, but in the main offenders were taken to the prison at Shepton Mallet where an execution chamber had been specially built and a British-style gallows erected. In the 29th Infantry Division there was only one serious incident during the whole of their stay. A woman was raped at Gunnislake. She was accosted whilst walking home from the Royal British Legion Hall, where she had been helping out that evening and tried to escape by joining another woman friend. She was hit and dragged into a field where the assault took place. The entire Division was paraded on Whitchurch Down the following day when the guilty man was identified by the woman's friend. He was Court Martialled at Plymouth and hanged by British hangman Albert Pierrepoint on 12th October 1944.

On a happier note, at least forty American soldiers married local girls. An example will illustrate the mood of those times: a charming and attractive young woman I will refer to as Rita (not her real name) was courted by a handsome American soldier we knew as 'Joe'. Poor Joe was madly in love and would pace up and down some distance from where Rita lived, unwilling to call because her mother was a rather fierce old lady. Eventually he would ask us boys to kindly go and see if Rita was coming out or not. One of us would run to the house, but before we got to the door an upstairs window would open and Rita's smiling face would appear with a whispered assurance she wouldn't be long. Another Tavistock lass was engaged to be married to an American soldier. Her fiancée survived the war and returned home with his unit, from where he sent her the cost of the fare to cross the Atlantic on the pride of the United States merchant fleet, the luxury liner SS *America*. It was a very happy marriage and she was able to visit her home town on several occasions afterwards. Most 'GI Brides' were packed onto crowded ships specially chartered for the trip and many of them did not find the idyllic 'home on the range' they had been led to expect. *'C'est la Vie!'*

In February 1944, the Supreme Allied Commander, General Dwight D. Eisenhower inspected 'H' Company of the 29th Division at Tavistock, followed by the Commander of 1st Army, Lt. Gen. Omar N. Bradley who came in March to address the officers of the Division. The American forces then became involved in more intensive training including 'Exercise Tiger' on Slapton Sands where the intended landings on the coast of France were rehearsed with live shelling and bullets. Just before D-Day, General Eisenhower and the overall Land Forces Commander, Lt. General Sir Bernard Montgomery, met at Abbotsfield House for a conference and today there is a memorial plaque in their honour, mounted over the fireplace in the room they used. I remember coming out of school one day at 4 p.m. and seeing crowds of people dispersing outside. You could never keep a secret for long in Tavistock and word had got out that our most famous General was at Abbotsfield, news that drew the crowds hoping for a glimpse of the great man and maybe General Eisenhower too. I think they were rewarded but I was just too late.

Right: General Omar Bradley, U.S. Army, addressing officers of the 29th Infantry Division on Whitchurch Down before 'D' Day 1944. (Courtesy Tavistock History Society)

Below: Memorial Plaque at Abbotsfield commemorating the meeting held there prior to 'D' Day between General Dwight D. Eisenhower and Field Marshall Lord Montgomery of Alamein. (Author's photo)

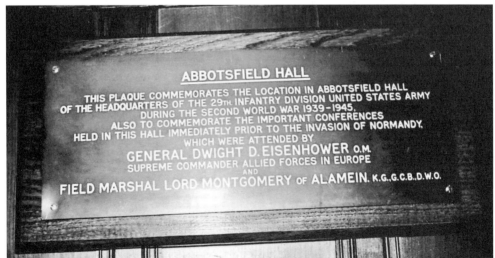

ABBOTSFIELD HALL

THIS PLAQUE COMMEMORATES THE LOCATION IN ABBOTSFIELD HALL OF THE HEADQUARTERS OF THE 29TH INFANTRY DIVISION UNITED STATES ARMY DURING THE SECOND WORLD WAR 1939-1945. ALSO TO COMMEMORATE THE IMPORTANT CONFERENCES HELD IN THIS HALL IMMEDIATELY PRIOR TO THE INVASION OF NORMANDY, WHICH WERE ATTENDED BY GENERAL DWIGHT D. EISENHOWER O.M. SUPREME COMMANDER ALLIED FORCES IN EUROPE AND FIELD MARSHAL LORD MONTGOMERY OF ALAMEIN. K.G.,G.C.B.,D.W.O.

General Dwight Eisenhower, Supreme Commander, inspects soldiers of the 29th Infantry Division in Bedford Square before 'D' Day 1944. (Courtesy of Tavistock History Society)

Suddenly the Americans were gone. One day (it must have been during May 1944) my cousin Roger called for me in a state of excitement. 'Come quickly' he said, 'the Yanks are leaving!' We hastened to Bedford Square and stood on the corner of the square and Plymouth Road. There were hundreds of townsfolk gathered to see them off. We did not have long to wait before they came marching down Whitchurch Road and over Abbey Bridge in a huge column (I think four abreast but cannot be sure) all with steel helmets, packs and rifles etc., ready for combat. They swung into Plymouth Road in silence. There was no cheering, no flag waving or bands, just the tramp tramp of their boots and subdued sobs from some of the girls. The soldiers looked straight ahead and maintained their dressing to perfection and I noticed their helmet straps were securely fastened instead of dangling carelessly like the ones we saw in the films. It was a sombre and business-like occasion. I do not know how many there were, but was afterwards told they were still coming from Down Road as the leading ranks reached Drakes Statue half a mile away. None of us knew where they were going but it was obvious something 'big' was about to happen and so it proved to be when, on 6th June, the great invasion was launched on the coasts of France. The 29th Division landed on 'Omaha' Beach and sustained massive loss of life.

On the day after D-Day my cousin Cora, who was in the WRENS, got married at Yelverton Roman Catholic Church. My grandfather gave her away as her father was at sea with the Royal Navy. The taxi taking them from Tavistock to the church got no further than Horrabridge, the road being completely blocked with American army lorries full of soldiers, and so they had to walk the two or three miles to Yelverton, mostly uphill and amid cheers and encouragement from the soldiers. How my elderly grandfather did it I will never know, but for many of the soldiers it was their last glimpse of civilian life before they died.

Three weeks later on 28th June, the first trainload of casualties, 292 of them, arrived at Tavistock, some with arms or legs missing, others with horrendous injuries. They were taken to the 115th Field Hospital. As the invading forces pushed inland more and more wounded men were admitted, another 292 in October, 589 during November, and 793 in December. Four hundred operations were performed after the December receptions. The last group of wounded men arrived on Christmas Day after a heavy snowstorm. The ambulances had trouble getting up the hill leading to the moor, and householders helped out by bringing ashes and cinders from their firesides to spread in front of them to give their tyres a grip on the icy surface.

As the fighting took place further and further inland on the Continent, other Field Hospitals were established closer to the front and the number of patients to Plaster Down diminished accordingly until finally, in April 1945, the unit was given advance warning to be prepared to move to France. The last patients were transferred to 112th Field Hospital at Newton Abbot and the 115th officially closed on 28th April. Then there was the task of packing all their medical and military equipment prior to the evacuation of Plaster Down on 23rd May 1945, when the unit left for France.

And so there ended an historic period in the history of Tavistock. Today there is no trace of the camp at Plaster Down – it has returned to its natural state of grass and ferns and heather. Whitchurch Down too is free of tents and lorries, and its unspoilt beauty is now as it always was. But those big-hearted young soldiers, with their gum and their good looks and friendliness, live on in the memories of those old enough to recall their stay. They were not all angels (no army has them) but they went and fought and died in a theatre of war that was not strictly theirs. The Japanese campaign was the American prime consideration. I do not detract for a moment from the efforts of our own army for whom I feel a great pride, but an emotional part of me is eternally grateful for the sacrifice of those men from another nation, namely the United States, whose bravery and resources tipped the balance in our favour and secured the Ultimate Victory in Europe.

Tavistock Goosey Fair

'...'eave down your prong
An' step it along
To Tavistock Goozey Vair'.

The first Tavistock market and fair was granted to the monks of the Abbey by King Henry I in 1105, as a mark of appreciation for their contribution towards the cost of a military campaign in Normandy. Future monarchs granted a total of five fairs to the town, one of which was the ancient Michaelmas Fair which dates from the early sixteenth century and was to become the annual Goose Fair of today. In those days the event was an important date in the calendar for buying and selling goods of all kinds as well as a farmer's market. Servants and field hands paraded on this day and made themselves available for hire and, of course, there were entertainments.

Today little has changed in principle. The farmers still have their market on that day, various traders have their stands and the people of Tavistock have their entertainments. For more than 100 years, there has been a Cattle Market in the town where sheep and cattle are auctioned and where a separate Poultry Market is held. Goose Fair Day is an important occasion for farmers when more store cattle are normally sold than at any other time of year and usually over 100 geese. When I was a boy, large numbers of cattle were transported to Tavistock on the GWR railway line and unloaded in a special siding just below the cattle market from where it was a short walk to the market. My sister Dilys remembers cattle being herded through the town and cowering in a doorway to dodge the hoofs and bobbing horns as they swept down Brook Street (the practice of 'de-horning' had not yet been introduced).

The second Wednesday in October – the fixed date for the event – is dominated by the fun fair and amusements supplemented by large numbers of stallholders or 'cheap-jacks' as my mother always called them. I remember the last funfair before the Second World War started. I was just five years old and the 'bumper cars' as they were known then (today's 'Dodgems') were situated in the meadows alongside the 'galloping horses' roundabout and various side shows. There was very little 'dodgems' going on – in fact, the idea seemed to be to bump as many other cars as possible and my Aunt Jane certainly upheld that tradition when she took me for a ride and crashed head on with another car; I was catapulted into the front framework of our car and split my lips in the process. The only other recollection I have of that year's event was watching a huge red steam traction engine, hissing and trembling as its whirling flywheel operated a drive belt, which in turn worked a generator to supply the power and lighting for the amusements. The same machine bore the inscription in gold lettering: 'Messrs Anderton and Rowland' who were, of course, the proprietors.

Goose Fair in Bedford Square 1950s. (Courtesy Mr T. Hicks, Tavistock)

There were not any such amusements during the war years and the occasion was limited to the farmer's market, I believe. The first Goose Fair after the ending of hostilities was in 1945, but on a limited scale – in fact, so limited the whole affair was contained in the Wharf area and part of Bedford Square.

The following year the attractions were more numerous and varied. The schools gave their pupils the day off (they still do) and Messrs. 'Whiteleggs' amusements dominated the proceedings over Anderton and Rowland who had been the leading fairground operators for decades. At the 2009 Goose Fair the author was fortunate in meeting Mr George Rowland DeVey who, with his brother, operates the fair today. He told me his father and two senior family members served in the armed forces during the Second World War and saw much active service. They had little enthusiasm for the business on their return and it went into decline. That gave Whitleggs the opportunity to take over some of their sites and replace them as the top fairground attraction until the late 1990s, when they went into liquidation. Anderton and Rowland then acquired their business to regain once more their premier position.

The first post-war fair included 'swing boats' and roundabouts in Bedford Square, 'bumper cars' in the wharf, and for the first time ever, a 'big wheel' in the meadows beside the bandstand. Along the bank below the canal were coconut 'shies', hoop-la

The 'Big Wheel'. (Photo reproduced from *Tavistock Goosey Fair* by permission of the author Guy Belsham)

stalls, and shooting ranges. One coconut 'shie' supplied customers with lightweight wooden balls about the size of a tennis ball, and I swear the coconuts were somehow glued to their containers because I only ever saw one or two toppled off by fit young men who hurled the missiles with all their might. My brother-in-law Ron Marks, a very fit young chap, was hit in the eye by a ball that re-bounded off the coconut he aimed at and gave him a 'shiner'. Nevertheless, on another occasion, he persevered and after more attempts than he can remember won a number of coconuts, too many to carry and kicked the surplus one along the path to his home in Brook Street.

The hoop-las consisted of a number of wooden square plinths about a foot high on which were fastened a tempting selection of prizes, but the rubber rings which the customers threw barely cleared the corners and had to land perfectly horizontal as they descended to embrace the plinths and qualify for a win. It was hardly 'all the fun of the fair'. The shooting galleries were the best as far as youngsters like me were concerned. Rifles operated by compressed air with crooked sights were aimed at a pyramid of empty tin cans and 'fired' corks. It was an irresistible challenge to the contestants. In later years the galleries became more traditional, with moving targets and air rifles that fired pellets.

Activities began at around 10 a.m. Townsfolk had the fair to themselves, until around 3 p.m., when farmers and their families came to enjoy themselves after attending the

Example of old fashioned 'bumper cars' or 'Dodgems'. (Courtesy of Dingles Fairground Heritage Centre, Milton Abbot, Devon)

cattle market. I remember them commandeering all the rides including the 'galloping horses' which were a firm favourite with them. Parents brought their young children at about that time. In early evening the buses from Plymouth and surrounding areas discharged further crowds who dominated the proceedings until they finished. Loud musical accompaniment and sirens signalling the ending of the rides rent the air and the noise was deafening. It continued well into the night when the sky over Tavistock glowed a crimson red, interspersed with white flashing lights and the noise level at its zenith. Residents in Plymouth Road and beyond just had to grin and bear it.

'Cheapjacks' lined Bedford Square and along the pavement to Abbey Bridge from early morning, hawking all manner of goods, from cheap jewellery to clothing and medicines with alleged magical healing powers for every complaint. One man held sway every year without fail on the corner of the Square and Duke Street. He was Phil Strong and, as his name suggests, was a fine figure of a man, tanned and rippling with muscles. Stripped to the waist in all weathers, with his upper body clad only in a sparkling white vest, he occupied an elevated box rather like a pulpit and exercised with a variety of chest expanders to attract attention. On a table in front were arrayed rows of small brown bottles containing a substance he referred to as 'Spanish Demiana'; I have since concluded this must have been a mild form of the well-known stimulant commonly called 'Spanish Fly'. When a sufficiently large crowd had assembled he would explain and extol its wonderful properties. 'This is what the Spanish ladies give their men to keep them fit and energetic' he would declare, adding with a lascivious grin: 'a good Spanish woman would kill half you men!' This would be followed by snickers of derision from the male onlookers and a tittering among the women present interspersed with 'tut, tuts' whilst we boys could only guess at what he was talking about (we were far more naïve than youngsters of today). Eventually, Mr Strong's compelling and amusing banter led to the more serious business of selling the stuff when his assistant (his wife I think), was hard pressed to keep up with the demand as outstretched hands from all sides proffered the half crowns (12.5p) each bottle cost. When all was done there would be a half hour break before the whole performance started again.

Then there were the 'china' men selling huge armfuls of china dinner services and a variety of china items from the back of a lorry. They always had London accents and their traditional 'Cockney' humour held their listeners' full attention with their wisecracks and breathtaking antics. For example, one of them would juggle a pile of crockery arranged in a pyramid, gently tilting them at an angle to make them clatter before tossing them into the air and catching them with a rattling sound that made

A fairground attraction of yesteryear. (Courtesy of Dingles Fairground Heritage Centre, Milton Abbot, Devon.

A thrilling ride seen at Tavistock Goose Fair 2009. (Author's photo)

you gasp. Never fear – they were caught expertly and I never saw a piece broken. This display would be accompanied by non-stop 'patter' extolling the value of the ridiculously low priced items on offer. The red-faced accomplice would smack his fist into his palm to emphasise how cheap their never-to-be-repeated offer was. 'I don't want fifteen pounds!' he would yell, 'or ten – take the ruddy lot for a fiver!' Often, if response was slow, he would put on a show of mock despair saying something like 'Blimey, what a lot of misers! Tell you what (I must be bloody mad!) 'ere take this lot on top' adding maybe a full tea set to the twenty-four-piece dinner set on offer. That did it. Soon a brisk trade was in progress and everyone was happy.

Yet another regular 'performer' set up a stall outside the Abbey Chapel. All he had was a trestle table with a big suitcase on it from which he attracted attention (he called it a sensation) by taking pocket watches from it and stuffing them into small brown padded packets and yelling for 'sporting men to have a gamble with me at only half a crown a time'. The 'gamble' was picking the right packet from a selection laid out on the table; if you didn't win a pocket watch you got a cheap piece of jewellery, which cost a fraction of the sum you paid him for being a 'sport'. Occasionally, he would shuffle just three packets in front of you, one of which you knew held a watch because you saw it being put in, but I never saw anyone choose the right one. It was cleverly done and good entertainment.

An old favourite survives! A 'Helter Skelter' at Goose Fair 2009. (Author's photo)

A similar act took place on the corner of Plymouth Road and the Bedford Hotel where a dark-skinned man wearing a huge hat with vertical stripes bawled 'Ah gotta horse!' over and over again. His gaudy appearance and hoarse cries soon attracted the attention he sought when numbered tickets would be offered to those who fancied some sport. A large board with numbered squares all over it was propped against the hotel railings. The idea was to purchase a ticket whose number matched one of those on the board, each of which had a cash prize marked up alongside the number. As you might expect the punters invariably paid more than the prizes were worth.

A sad display of another kind took place for two or three years running on the corner of Pepper Street and Duke Street by a wiry little man accompanied by his wife, both of them in their sixties I should think. They were very old fashioned, the wife dressed in black and bare headed, the old boy in a frayed jacket, waistcoat and a shirt without a collar. He wore a large wide-brimmed hat which he removed to reveal an imposing mass of grey hair above a wrinkled forehead and unshaven lined face. He would challenge anyone to tie him up with a length of rope from which he would endeavour to escape; in fact, he was quite good and usually managed to get free after a great show of struggling and gasping, when his wife would pass his hat for the spectators to make a donation. The last time I saw his act, two Royal Marine Commandos stepped forward (servicemen in uniform were a common sight in Tavistock for years after the war ended) and one of them took up the challenge. A worried old lady watched as her spouse was turned on his belly and trussed like the proverbial chicken with his hands securely fastened to his ankles behind his back. But that was not all; an ingenious loop of rope encircled his neck in such a way that the more he fought to get free the tighter the noose became. In no time he was writhing and rolling all over the place, with his face turning blue and eyes bulging so that the wife ignored his shaking head and begged for him to be released, which he was. It was a degrading sight made worse when hardly anyone put a donation into the hat.

By far the most popular and well patronised event was a boxing booth, where two or three professional fighters challenged all comers to last three one-minute rounds with any one of them. The contests took place in a marquee situated in the dip to the right of and on the far side of the little bridge you drive across before the main entrance to what is now the Tavistock main car park. The car park then was the Bedford Hotel garden and was separated from the wharf by a high stone wall. The wharf was an empty and convenient area in which to hold some of the fair, with a large entrance leading to the meadows where 'Meadowlands' now is. There was a full size ring inside the boxing tent but no seating; it was standing room only but nobody complained and the place was always packed. An admission fee was paid on entry and those contenders who lasted the challenge got a share of the proceeds from a collection after the fight. There were never any shortage of challengers, mainly servicemen but occasionally local lads, and the contests were generally very good with no-one getting seriously hurt (the 'professionals' soon sized up their opponents and either disposed of them quickly or, if they were good, allowed them to ride out the three rounds and provide the spectators with some sport).

There were other niceties for us children, to which we were totally unaccustomed. Toffee apples, for example, were sold from a stall with a steaming cauldron of what I imagine was some kind of toffee mixture, into which small green apples (cookers from the taste of them) on little sticks were dipped and put on display and to cool. You needed a cast-iron stomach to enjoy them. The biggest disappointment as far as I was concerned was the first candy floss I ever had. It looked delicious on its thin wooden holder with a huge mass of wavering pink 'floss' wrapped around it but to my disgust it was mostly diffused air and the taste was barely recognisable. In any case, however careful you were, it left a sticky deposit all over your face.

The aftermath of all this was the litter which had to be cleared and the mud-bath in the meadows caused by the trample of thousands of pairs of feet (it always seemed to rain on Goose Fair Day). The council workers earned the admiration of us all for the way the place was restored to its natural beauty soon afterwards. As with the children of today, the fair was a topic of conversation for days afterwards, and the dubious transactions we saw and often took part in were overshadowed by the good times we had. There were not any 'theme parks' in those days and Goose Fair was an attraction (apart from the occasional visit by a travelling circus) that brought the citizens of Tavistock together for mutual fun and enjoyment. Long may it be so.

My mother and grandmother knew the following old song and used to sing it to me when I was a small child. The tune has a jolly lilt to it quite in keeping with the words. I don't suppose many youngsters in Tavistock today have ever heard it but it should be preserved as a reminder of the time when ordinary country folk had that rare pleasure of a day off from their labours on Fair Day. Here are the words in full:

'Tavistock Goozey Vair'

'Tis just a month come Vriday next
Bill Champerdown an'me
Us drove 'cross ole Dartimoor
The Goozey Vair to zee.
Us made ourselves quite vitty
Us shaved an' grazed our 'air,
An' off us goes in our Sunday clothes
Behind ole Bill's grey mare.

Us smelled the sage an' onions
All the way from Whitchurch Down
An' didn't us 'ave a blow out
When us put up in town.
An' there us met Ned 'Annaford
Jan Steer and Nicky Square
An'it seemed to we
All Devon must be
At Tavistock Goozey Vair.

CHORUS
'Tis all then where be gwain
An' what be doin' aught there,
'Eave down yer prang
An' step it alang
To Tavistock Goozey Vair.

Us went an' seed the 'osses
An the yaffers an' the yaws
Us went 'pon all the roundabouts
An' into all the shaws
An' then it started rainin'
An blowin' to us face
An' so us goes up to the Rose
An' 'as a dish o'tay.

An' then us 'ad a sing-song
An' folks kept droppin' in
An' them what knows us all came 'round
An' 'ad a drop of gin.
Till what with one an' 'tother
Us didn't seem to care
Whether us was up on Bellever Tor
Or Tavistock Goozey Vair.

The view towards Abbey Bridge Goose Fair Day 1950s. (Courtesy Mr T. Hicks, Tavistock)

CHORUS

'Twas rainin straimes
An' dark as pitch
When us started 'ome that night
An' us 'adn't got past Merrivale Bridge
When the mare 'er took a fright.
Says Oi to Bill be careful
Or e'll 'ave us in the drains
Says 'ee to me
Begad says 'ee
Why 'ain't ee got the reins?

Just then the mare runs slap agin
A wacking gert big stone,
An' 'er kicked the trap to flippets
An' 'er trotted off alone.
When us came to, us reckoned
'Twas no good sittin' thar
So us 'ad to walk 'ome thirteen mile
From Tavistock Goozey Vair.

Tavistock Shops

In the Period Before, During, and After the Second World War

Parkwood Road

- **Parkwood Garage** (opposite entrance to Sunshine Terrace).
- **Greaves** Grocers (opposite old foundry). There was a small sweet factory at the back.
- **Minhinnick Dairy** (adjoining Greaves).

Vigo Bridge/Junction with Brook Street

- **Frost** Greengrocers.

Vigo Bridge/Junction with Parkwood Road

- **Bonds Garage** (also Ford dealers).

Brook Street (south side)

- **Young's** Second-hand goods and scrap yard.
- **Miss Redman's** Second-hand shoes, Clothes etc.
- **Dyas** Grocers.

In alleyway leading to Paul's Almhouses

- **Skinners** Bakery.
- **Bunsford** Shoe repairs.

Brook Street (south side cont'd.)

- **Rawbones** Drapers.
- **Pearce** China shop.
- **Barrett** Grocers.
- **Gale** Men's hairdresser.

Brook Street (north side)

- **Haimes** Grocers (opposite Frosts).
- **Burch** Wireless shop and servicing.

In alleyway adjacent to Tavistock Hotel

- **Burch** side entrance.
- **Sargeants** Wholesaler.

Brook Street (north side cont'd.)

- **Tavistock Hotel.**
- **Wilkins** Shoe shop.
- **Muzzlewhite** Grocers.
- **Miss Lugg** Sweet shop.
- **Ireland** Shoe shop.
- **Lily Rooke** Women and childrens wear.
- **Wadge** Photographer.
- **Bawden** Antique furniture, china, pictures etc.
- **Poole's** Fish and chip shop and café.
- **Gimlet** Photographer.
- **Miss Wooten** Sweet shop.
- **Ryall** Haberdashery.

Paddons Row

- **Blacksmith/Farrier** (name not known).
- **Hoare** Ladies and gents hairdressing.
- **Owens Dairy.**
- **White Hart public house.**

Exeter Street

- **Barkell** Tobacco, sweets, etc.
- **British Restaurant** on upper floor of Congregational Church.
- **Umbrella shop** at bottom of the street (name not known).

View of Town Hall (right) and Duke Street. Note the Congregational Church steeple. (Courtesy Tavistock History Society)

Duke Street (south side)

- **Creber** High class grocers (junction of entrance to Market Road and Duke Street).
- **Miss Watts** Tea rooms.
- **Palmer** Butcher.
- **Woolworths.**
- **Muzzlewhites** Paints and wallpaper.
- **Matthews Garage.**
- **Woolacott** Butcher and greengrocer.
- **Moore** Homemade cake shop and tea room.
- **Gribble** Jeweller.
- **Pillars** Newsagent.
- **Wool shop** (owner not known).
- **Barkell** Confectioner and tobacconist.
- **Roland Bailey** Florist and greengrocer.

Duke Street (north side)

- **Ingersons corner shop** Baker.
- **Unknown shop.**
- **World Stores.**
- **Boots** Chemist.

Pepper Street

- **Rendezvous** Ladies hairdresser.
- **John Westcott** Coal merchant.

Duke Street (north side cont'd)

- **Ganes** Shoes.
- **B & A** Butcher (later **Dewhurst**).
- **International Stores.**
- **Newmarket Hotel.** (When the hotel closed it was the site of the **HBSC Bank.** At the time of writing it is an estate agents office).
- **Perratons** Baker, cake shop and café. When Perratons closed it was the site of the **National Westminster Bank.**

Corner of Duke Street and Drake Road

- **Midland Bank.** At the time of writing it is the **HBSC Bank.**

Drake Road

- **Phillips** Bakery and cake shop.

Corner of Drake Road and Bedford Square

- Lloyds Bank.

East Corner of North Street

- Barclays Bank

North Street

- **F. C. Palmer** Grocer and off-licence.

Corner of North Street and Kilworthy Hill

- *Tavistock Gazette* Office and printing.

West Corner of North Street and West Street

- **Baker** Ironmongers, kitchen ware, etc.

Market Street (east side)

- **Martin's** Chemist.
- **Richards's** Hairdresser.
- **Millbay Laundry** (shop only).
- **Cole** Baker and tea room.
- **Eastman's (B. & A.)** Butcher.
- **Madame da Costa** Hairdresser.
- **Corner shop** (name not known) Toys.

(across the road same side)

- **Manchester House** (Co-op)
- **Trustee Savings Bank**
- **Ron Williams** Toys etc.
- **Co-op** Groceries
- **Co-op** Butcher
- **Co-op** Bakery (under the archway)
- **Coyles** Butcher

Market Street (west side)

- **Williams** Paints and wallpaper.
- **Ladies clothes shop** (name not known)
- **James** Newsagents (later **Pillars**).
- **Pearce** Chemist.
- **Kerswill** Paints and wallpaper.
- **Co-op** Household furniture.
- **Bates** Shoe repairs.
- **Thompson** Hairdresser.

Taylor Square

- *Tavistock Times* Office and printing.

Bannawell Street

- **Mrs. Worth** General store (opposite the chapel).

King Street (east side)

- Small private subscription library.

King Street (west side)

- **The ('Old') Cinema** formerly the Corn Market.
- **Fulfords** Agricultural merchants.
- **Wilton** Baker.
- **Annie Acton's pasty shop** (later moved to the cattle market).
- **Ellis** Bread, cakes, pasties etc. (replaced Annie Acton's) and afterwards moved to West Street.

Corner of Madge Lane

- **Small fish and chip shop** (name not known).

West Street (south side)

- **Jeffrey** Florist and greengrocer.
- **Willis** Butcher.
- **Lennards** Shoe shop.
- **Fellowes** Book shop.
- **Symons** Optician.
- **London House (Messrs. Sweets)** Ladies and children's clothing.
- **Miss Read** Ladies clothing.
- **Pearce's Café** (later **The Cozy Café**).
- **Holman & Ham** Chemist.
- **Underwoods** Groceries.

Corner of West Street and Russell Street

- **Gas Showroom.**

West Street (south side cont'd)

- **Langs** Fresh Fish shop (later **Pooles**).
- **Kerslake** Paints and Wallpaper.
- **Friend** Pork butcher famous for his sausages.
- **Chenhall** Bicycles, Prams etc. and repairs
- **Verran** Photographer.

- **White** Butcher.
- **The Church Hall** now a residential area.

West Street (north side)

- **Norman Brown** Baker and Confectioner.
- **Fellowes** Sports shop and Tobacconist.
- **C. V. Halford Thompson** Radio and Electrical.
- **Sweets** Gents' Outfitter.
- **Sweets** Toys, Sweets, Tobacco and Hairdressing.
- **Hepworths** Men's Tailors.
- **Queens Head Hotel.**
- **Mills** Jeweller.
- **Nicholson-Hill** Paints and Wallpapers.
- **Grigsby** Carpets and Furnishing.
- **Greaves** Radio, Batteries etc.
- **Solomon** Jeweller.
- **Townsend** Newsagent.

Looking down West Street. (Courtesy Tavistock History Society)

Ford Street (junction of Ralphs Court)

- **Bert Davey** Groceries.
- **Daisy Giles's 'Little Shoppe'.** Post Office, Sweets, Tobacco, etc.

Plymouth Road

- Carrs Garage.

West Bridge (at 64 West Bridge cottages)

- **Miss Brenton** Sweets, Tobacco, etc.

Memories fade after more than sixty years and consequently some of the above names may be wrongly spelt. The order in which they are named may also not be correct. I can assure the reader, however, that I have personal recollection of nearly all of them. My cousin, the late Mrs Glenda Harvey (*nee* Roberts), and her husband Den very generously spent much time reminiscing to supply the list given above.

The Shops I Knew

Frosts

I knew Mr and Mrs Frost from my earliest age. My mother was a regular customer for many years and purchased all her greengrocery items from them. They also sold tobacco and cigarettes, but during the war years only regular customers were sold these items as a limited quantity was allowed. Mr and Mrs Frost were kindly and cheerful people who had a plot of land at the top of Green Lane where they grew a lot of the vegetables they sold in the shop. It must have been hard work doing this and running the shop as well, which makes their success all the more admirable.

Bonds Garage

The business was owned by two brothers, both of whom were devout Methodists. It was a very prosperous concern, selling petrol, new and used cars, and with a workshop for repairs and servicing. My most vivid memory of Bonds is being sent there by my mother for a pint of paraffin, used to light the fire in winter months. A used lemonade bottle was duly filled at one of the hand operated pumps for a copper or two (I doubt it would be permitted today). My mother, who always seemed to have a problem lighting a fire, would sprinkle a lavish amount onto the firewood and coal and throw in a lighted match after which the flames would roar up the chimney. The wonder of it was we never had a house fire as a result!

Young's

There is nothing new about recycling – Young's recycled paper, glass, wood; in fact, anything that could be saved was saved during the Second World War and afterwards. Their yard, which was situated next to Frosts, was extensive and occupied the area from Brook Street to the bank of the River Tavy, all of it cobbled. The firm sold second-hand furniture, china and glassware as well as wood for burning. A little man I only ever knew as Archie operated a huge circular saw to cut branches into logs and the noise, a high pitched screaming, could be heard all along Brook Street. I often watched Archie performing this task when buying a sack of logs for my mother and flinched as the whirring saw did its work; when the blade suddenly broke through, his outstretched arms with hands clasping the wood on either side would leap apart as if on a spring. There was no guard or goggles or protective clothing.

Archie could be seen at times all over the town pushing a handcart with various items piled upon it, either for delivery or destined for the yard. Mr Young was an elderly man with a shock of white hair and a military style moustache twirled at the ends into points. He was an old soldier who had served on the Afghan borders (nothing has changed!) and in the Boer War. He played the bass drum in the Salvation Army band and his younger brother, who too had fought on the Afghan frontier and in South Africa, played the kettle drum. The business was run by the older Mr Young, a very kindly, friendly man who lived just a step away further along Brook Street with his wife and son.

On one occasion when I was in my teens, I was closing a deal with Mr Young and was going up the granite steps to his office, when I noticed a water colour painting on top of a bale of waste paper. It was a seascape and the raindrops were blowing onto it which I thought was a shame. I asked Mr Young if I could have it and offered to pay him. 'Give me half-a-crown' he said, 'and good luck'. It was twenty or more years before I could afford to have that picture framed after lying out of sight among my possessions all that time. The person who did the work pointed out the artist had signed the painting 'R. Chappell' and was almost certainly Reuben Chappell of Falmouth, who had been a prolific painter of schooners entering and leaving Falmouth harbour. This was confirmed a year or two later by an authority in Exeter, when I learned it is worth a far larger sum than what I gave for it. I like the picture now just as much as I did then and will never sell it.

Dyas

General groceries and green groceries. A very pleasant couple ran this shop and both were devout Christians. Mr Dyas was a 'conscientious objector' during the Second World War and was heavily criticised for it; mostly by women whose husbands were away with the armed forces. They probably lost a lot of custom as well because of it. Personally, I thought it was a brave act of principle.

Crebers

I remember when this shop was run by Mr Norman Creber, a slim energetic man, very polite and just the sort of person to have charge of a family business such as this. He used to process their own brand of coffee and, when doing so, the lovely aroma spread as far as Bedford Square and Vigo Bridge, depending on which direction the wind came from. The shop has grown since my young days but the quality of their goods remains unchanged – the best there is.

Palmers

A family butcher before the start of the Second World War and still going strong. His son John was in my class at Tavistock Grammar School when all the boys marvelled at his physique, tall and big and strong with a hairy chest and tree trunk legs. He was a mild mannered individual with leadership qualities. I well remember my first Army Cadet Camp on Salisbury plain. I was very immature at that time and tried to dodge the chores I had been allotted –washing pots and pans after evening meal. I wanted to go into Warminster and was actually making for the camp entrance when John Palmer appeared. He didn't waste words arguing and I found myself being dragged back to my place of work, and gently but firmly told 'to get on with it'. When it was done he gave me a wry smile saying 'Right James! Now you can go into Warminster'. I recall a geography lesson conducted by 'Dicky' Dymond (described affectionately in my Schooldays Part 2). 'Dicky' was a small man with grey hair and spectacles, normally very dignified and mild mannered but on this occasion 'Big John Palmer' had gone too far and upset our tutor who, in the only outburst of exasperation I ever witnessed from him, threatened to give Palmer 'a jolly good thrashing'. The whole class lost their self control and laughed without restraint, upon which 'Dicky' left the room and did not return, leaving us shamefaced and contrite.

Woolworths

When I was a boy the sign above the doors said: 'Woolworths 3d. & 6d. Stores'. I always wanted one of their ice creams which, in the period before hostilities commenced with Germany, was stored in cylindrical lengths and cut to order. For 3d. you got a stick of vanilla flavoured ice cream inserted into a cone, from which you had to peel away a paper wrapping, all very hygienic and the product lost none of its flavour in the process. When the war began, ice cream disappeared for almost six years. Now Woolworths has disappeared and that is a sad loss.

Haimes

This little shop was opposite Frosts next door to my gran's house, and as a very small boy I was often sent there for some item or other. I recall Mr Haimes preparing weekly rations for his customers during the war, religiously weighing cheese or lard, for example, on a brass scale lined with greaseproof. Tiny scrapes of the latter were carefully added until the scales tipped. He was a quiet man of mature years, with spectacles, and always wore a brown dust coat. His wife wore a white apron and had white hair above an ever smiling face; both of them were very kind to me.

Tavistock Hotel

A very popular meeting place for male residents of Brook Street. Pubs were places for social gatherings in those days before they were turned into mini restaurants. There was a covered alleyway at the side with a side entrance, to what I can only describe as a standing room only cubicle, unheated and cheerless. Entry was up two granite steps and through a door into a sort of cubby hole, with a stone floor and no decoration whatsoever. Halfway up the inside wall was a wooden hatch which you tapped to get attention. The landlord served you from the bar itself. I often went there to buy cigarettes for my father, but it was mainly used by women who would not dream of going into such a place unaccompanied, seeking a quiet tipple (or two), which they drank standing.

Wilkins

The last in a row of shops and next door to the Tavistock Hotel. Mr Wilkins was an elderly, very smartly dressed man who always stood in the doorway greeting passers-by, most of whom were customers of his. My grandfather often told me how, as a young man, he went to Wilkins shoe shop and ordered a pair of John White made to measure boots. He wore boots all his life (black for weekdays, brown for Sunday) and never owned a pair of shoes.

Bawdens

Mr Bawden invested heavily in antique furniture and various bric-a-brac. Apart from his shop, a large establishment that extended all the way back to Exeter Street, he had two warehouses packed with goods – one adjacent to the bottom of Brooklands Drive, and another in Mount Tavy Road opposite the entrance to Green Lane, both of which have since been developed for housing. He was a short middle-aged man with horned rimmed glasses and a moustache who spent a lot of time standing in the entrance to his Brook Street shop, greeting people he knew. On each side were huge glass windows, extending some way from the front to the entrance proper and forming a sort of arcade. This site has also been developed recently. His son married my Council School teacher Miss Moon.

Pooles

Apart from the small fish and chip shop at the bottom of Madge Lane (which was never a competitor) Pooles was the only fish and chip shop in Tavistock until after the end of the Second World War when a rival establishment (Ives fish and chip shop) opened further along Brook Street. During the war years, it was always packed with people queuing for counter service or waiting for a place in the café at the rear. Mr and Mrs Poole were very pleasant people who worked hard for their success. I have seen customers standing shoulder to shoulder, waiting their turn and overflowing into the street. A great number of them were soldiers or sailors seeking refreshment after a few pints of beer. There wasn't much choice for the fish, but it always came hot and freshly cooked. In the café, you got a plate of fish and chips with bread and butter and a cup of tea for half-a-crown or less.

When peace came, Mr Poole handed over the business to his brother and his wife, whilst he and Mrs Poole took over the fresh fish shop in West Street.

Ives

Mr Ives was a Yorkshire man who opened for business at the end of the war. His was a modest establishment, with bare wooden flooring and just him running the show. He was a kind man who sometimes gave away small bags of chips to children who could not afford to buy. They became faithful customers later on, and Mr Ives made a lot of friends.

Hoare

Ladies and men's hairdressers. Most men had their hair cut, on average, every other week, and Saturday mornings at Hoare's saw a packed shop with customers seated on black couches on a raised platform, watching the performance and sharing the local gossip. Inside half an hour you got to hear about all the scandals and developments in Tavistock and district. The air was blue with cigarette smoke and the atmosphere was cheerfully relaxing. When it was your turn Mr Hoare, who I believe was brother to another Mr Hoare who was manager of the mill in Parkwood Road, would ask 'and how would you like it cut?' or words to that effect, but no matter what you said you got the same haircut as everyone else – 'short back and sides'. It was strictly men only in there, as it was for ladies only in their salon, which no man dared or dreamed of entering for any reason whatsoever. Women with young sons would gently open the door to where the men were and say something like 'can I leave young Billy (or Harry or Michael) with you Mr Hoare?' to which he would glance around the shop and perhaps say 'Yes Mrs___ come and collect him in half an hour'. Mr Hoare's son Dennis was a walking recommendation for his father's business, with his copious, jet black hair sleeked back in a shiny mass above a rounded, good-looking face.

Owens Dairy

The shop was situated between Hoare's and the White Hart Hotel, and sold the usual dairy products. In Paddons Row they kept a horse-drawn milk cart for delivering their goods to customer's homes. I vividly remember a girl called Pat Fricker (I think) who drove the two wheeled float, which looked more like a Roman chariot than a delivery vehicle. She used to rein in the horse at the entrance to Brooklands and back up facing the drive, before flicking her whip and rattling the reins to get the animal surging forward to breast the steep driveway, and God help anyone who got in the way! Thankfully, no-one ever did.

Boots

This shop was a regular port of call for several of us boys because it had a second floor that stocked books and foreign stamps. Most of us collected stamps and were attracted to the little packets containing (unused) stamps from all over the world. I learned a lot of geography as a result.

B & A Butchers

This business was to become part of the Dewhurst Empire in later years. My mother was a customer for many years when the working manager was a Mr Flood. When I walked home from the Council School during the war I often paused at the window to be entertained by the gruesome sight of Mr Flood skinning a rabbit (rabbits were a welcome addition to the weekly meat rations). I would watch in fascination as the feet were neatly chopped off, followed by some nifty knife work on the underside of the animal and around its neck. Then, with great skill, the furry skin was peeled back from the rear to the head revealing a startlingly pink body underneath, and a pink head with glaring eyes. Strangely, the sights I often witnessed did nothing to spoil my enjoyment of rabbit pie, for example.

Perratons

A large and very successful establishment situated in Bedford Square next to the Newmarket Hotel. The front part was a shop, selling bread and all kinds of confectionery. The back area was a cafeteria style tea shop and was very well patronised all year round. When still at school, I did some part-time work for the owner, Mr Cotton, at his home in Kilworthy Hill. I cut his grass lawn and weeded some flowerbeds, for which I was rewarded with a sum of money and regular stops for tea and cakes. He was an exceptionally kind and generous man with a ready smile. I believe he died in middle age when his son took over running the business. At the time of writing, the place is the office of an estate agent.

F. C. Palmer grocers and off-licence

It was an old fashioned shop with a huge mahogany counter and brass scales. They catered for a rather 'select' clientele whose purchases were delivered by an elderly Mr

Hocking on and old style delivery bike. He always wore a cap and brown dust coat. I believe it was the only job he ever had, starting straight from school and working well into middle age, until Mr Palmer died.

Bakers

A thriving ironmongery business, which today we would refer to as a hardware shop. The shop was large with an old fashioned mahogany counter and a storeroom at the back. They seemed to sell everything you needed for the home. Mr Baker knew everybody and had a good sense of humour, as illustrated by the following story related to me by someone who witnessed it.

Among the products at Pitts Cleave quarry were reinforced concrete posts made in wooden open topped boxes rather like coffins. The art lay in smoothing the finished product level with the edges so as to match the other three sides, and which had to be checked with a spirit level. One day a new boy, not long out of school, was told by the foreman to cycle in to Bakers and buy a new bubble for a spirit level. An unsuspecting youngster duly entered the shop where he was served by Mr Baker. 'Who sent you here for this?' he asked, and on hearing the man's name nodded knowingly. 'Wait here sonny' and he was gone. In no time he was back with a small glass bottle filled with water up to the neck. 'Now my boy' he said, turning the bottle upside down and pointing to the bubble, 'just you tell your foreman from me there is a bubble and if he can bloody well get it out he can have it with my compliments'. Those were the days!

Bakers Ironmongers, now a pasty shop and café. (Courtesy Tavistock History Society)

Willis

Family butcher, and a popular one. Mr Willis was a big man with a cheerful smile for his customers. He was Mayor of Tavistock in 1949 (I think) when the Queen, who was at that time still the Princess Elizabeth, paid a visit and he had the honour to greet her in Guildhall Square. His son attended the Grammar School at the same time as me where he was affectionately known to his classmates as 'Willy'. He was a talented swimmer and always won the diving competition at the annual school swimming sports, held each year at the Bannawell Street baths.

Friend's

Mr Friend was famous in the Tavistock district for his sausages, which were made on the premises; I have seen queues on a Friday morning stretching from his shop door all the way down West Street and around the corner of Russell Street, nearly as far as the old Wesleyan Chapel.

Norman Brown

Cakes and confectionery. As related elsewhere, he was one of two tradesmen who sold ice cream after the war. He purchased or rented one of two Nissen Huts in the meadows after the war (where Meadowlands now is) and opened a café there in the summer months.

Sweets

Owned and managed by two brothers, one of whom had charge of men's outfitters. All the Whitchurch 'toffs'* purchased their outfits there, including made to measure suits etc. and every accessory from hats to socks, shirts, ties and raincoats.

Whitchurch was the most fashionable area to reside in after Down Road and just after the end of the Second World War every other house, it seemed, was occupied by a retired Colonel, Rear Admiral or Squadron Leader. They wrote letters to the local newspapers signed with their name, rank and decorations to give greater effect to what they had to say.

The well-known 'Tommy' Sweet ran the confectionery, tobacco and toy shop next door. It was the largest and best establishment of its kind in Tavistock. For a time, there was a men's barber shop at the rear manned by Jack Saunders. Jack was a manly character of mature years and a chain smoker. He cut your hair more or less as you wanted. I well recall standing in the rain, just before the first Christmas after the war ended, gazing into the toy shop window ablaze with lighting and well stocked with toys I could never hope to have. One was an electric train set (the first I ever saw) laid out on a track that spanned the entire display, complete with a station and a tunnel. The train ran continuously, to the delight and a lot of envy on the part of me and other young boys.

As already related, the Sweets also owned London House on the opposite side of the street which was a fashionable ladies clothing shop, and where my Aunt Mary worked for many years. Tommy Sweets were represented at shows and events all over the country and my aunt, as a long serving and reliable assistant, often travelled with the firm to help.

'Farmer Hard Times'

This chapter would not be complete without mention of this remarkable character. His real name I believe was Cox, and he farmed on the outskirts of the town on the Okehampton road. Nothing was ever satisfactory for him – if it was wet weather, he could do with some sunshine; if it was sunny, a little rain would do no harm; in short nothing was ever right for 'Hard Times Cox'. He sold his dairy products all over Tavistock with the aid of a bicycle, which had a rectangular metal milk float fastened to the side of it with a wheel to support it. At the back was a metal bar with hooks, from which hung a selection of various sized ladles, swaying and tinkling as he negotiated every bump in the road (I can imagine what present day environmental health officials would have to say about that!). My grandparents were customers of his all their lives; every night before retiring my grandfather would put a jug on the doorstep, covered with a saucer and with the right amount of money on top for payment. When he retired and moved to another part of the town the routine remained the same but each morning he would be standing at the gate, jug in hand, to greet Mr Cox and take delivery of the milk which was ladled from the float after removing the cover. Mr Cox is to be admired for his fortitude and initiative.

The Pannier Market

Although I have included separately a brief history of Tavistock market, this section would not be complete without some observations about the place when I was a boy, before and after the war years. The Pannier market then was a real traditional market place, not a mixture of bazaar and antique fair as it is today. Real farmer's wives in crisp white aprons attended their stalls all day patiently selling eggs, home-made butter, cheese and garden produce of every kind. Everything was wrapped in greaseproof paper and weighed on scales before you. It was a great social occasion when my Gran, for instance, was able to renew acquaintance with people she knew in and around the town amid a babble of voices and cheerful smiling faces. Older women always seemed to wear mainly black dresses, shoes, stockings and hats which were sometimes made of straw but always with a brim adorned with imitation flowers, and very smart they looked. Silver brooches twinkled and the talk was all broad Devon and music to my ears. Other stallholders sold matches, buttons, darning wool (do housewives still darn socks and pullovers I wonder?), cotton, needles; in fact, all the necessary odds and ends without which life would have been nigh impossible in the days when ordinary women made do with 'make and mend'.

Farmers were to be seen too, wearing flat caps or 'pork pie' hats, striped shirts and ties, tweed jackets which seemed too tight over wide shoulders and backs, corduroy or 'cavalry twill' trousers and brown gaiters over brown boots, each item highly polished. Typically they were thick-set men, stout with broad red faces and huge fists, many of them carrying a stick or sometimes a crook. Several of them transported their wives and wares to Tavistock by pony and trap; the few who had cars drove battered Fords or Vauxhalls. To sum up, nearly everybody paid a visit to the Pannier market on Fridays to pick up a bargain, maybe, but most certainly to pick up the latest gossip as well.

It will come as a surprise to most Tavistock residents to learn the Plymouth based *Western Morning News* was produced in a rented portion of the Pannier Market for a time. In March 1941, Plymouth suffered night after night of intensive bombing during the course of which their premises were badly damaged, cutting off their gas, electricity and water supplies. The paper transferred production to Exeter, temporarily, and then to Tavistock. After extensive alterations to the market, the necessary equipment was moved from Cattedown and in the nick of time, as the building it was stored in was destroyed the very next day. Newsprint was housed at Kit Hill and the Editorial staff, with their telegraph system, worked from rooms above a local bank. Some of them were accommodated in the town and my Gran had one of them, a lodger called 'Bunny' (which could only have been a nickname!) who was on the staff of the newspaper, and being a very pleasant fellow, he was remembered with affection years afterwards. Production started on 26th May 1941 and continued until 1944 when, after the 'D' Day landings and the continuing Allied successes, it was safe to return to their Plymouth base at Harmsworth House (named after the Proprietor Sir Harold Harmsworth who lived at Yelverton) which, incidentally, was the only building left standing in Frankfort Street. The late Mr Ken Doble, who was a seventeen-year-old Trainee Reporter, recalled travelling to and from Tavistock from Plymouth every day throughout that period, leaving at 4 p.m. and returning home by coach at 1.30 a.m., but often arriving back later through being delayed by enemy action.

At one time or another I had dealings with practically every businessman in the town but those described above represent the most well-known. Every purchase was paid for in cash. Bank cards and credit facilities simply did not exist; but on some occasions, I have known kind gestures by some of them towards regular customers, who were allowed to pay by two or three instalments for expensive items. It was appreciated by the customers and good for business.

Later in life, when I worked as a junior reporter for the *Tavistock Times*, my job entailed attending various social events, council meetings, the magistrates' court, balls and concerts in the Town Hall and so on. There, to my surprise, I found some of the shopkeepers I have described. I recall entering the lounge bar of the Bedford Hotel (a very 'upmarket' establishment in those days) to make some enquiries and seeing two very modest shop owners sipping their drinks and 'dressed to kill', as the saying went. Another time I witnessed one of the best known tradesmen in Tavistock making a fool of himself at a ball, where every man wore a dinner jacket and bow tie, it being an occasion of note. The Town Hall resounded with his raucous laughter and disapproving glances were cast in his direction as he struggled to keep his balance; it was a far cry from the figure I was familiar with, serving customers in his little shop. It was not the only time I saw this man letting himself down publicly, yet he is remembered now with respect and some adulation. Others became Town Councillors, members of Committees and Chairmen of some, where they did a good job guiding the town along the way to the prosperous place it is today. The lesson I learned was to the effect that all I have described was what 'made the world go around'. So it remains to this day, and I have no argument with that.

Leisure (Part 1)

What did we do in our spare time all those years ago and what entertainment did we have? This question revives many happy memories, despite the fact that television had not been invented, neither had computers and neither were there transistor radios or the like. A child of today would find it hard to be occupied or entertained in the way we were, but I can truthfully say it was certainly not the case at the time and, looking back, I cannot recall ever feeling bored except when I was very small and it was raining too heavily to go out to play. On such occasions my mother would often sprinkle some breadcrumbs outside our window and I would sit and watch the birds. Come to think of it, this was a wise move on my mother's part because I soon got to identify many different types of birds and my affection for them remains to this day.

A good starting point for this section is my reading. All my life I have been an avid reader, beginning with the child's ABC learning book my grandmother gave me to read at bedtime, as previously related. From there, I graduated to cartoon strips as soon as I learned to read at school, in particular the Rupert series in the *Daily Express* which my Gran unfailingly read as soon as the paper was delivered. Before long, I was borrowing small booklets from the children's section of the subscription library in King Street which my grandfather used. My favourite stories were seagoing adventures and one book stands out from all the rest. It was called 'The Spanish Main' by the immortal Captain Marryat (I think). It was about a boy just like me, who was befriended by an adventurer, who called himself Rapier and, as the name suggests, was an expert with that weapon. They went to sea together and faced pirates, shipwreck and of course, performed heroic deeds on an island inhabited by unfriendly savages. Then my mother treated me to the comic papers *Beano* one week and *Dandy* the next. I was enthralled with the doings of 'Desperate Dan' who had bristles all over his chin and ate his Aunt Aggie's cow pies; 'Keyhole Kate' a girl with glasses and a pointed nose, who was forever poking her nose into other people's business; then there was 'Lord Snooty and his Pals' an aristocratic leader of a boisterous gang getting up to all sorts of mischief; 'Hungry Horace' was another favourite with an appetite the notorious 'Billy Bunter' would have envied – and many more. Besides these two periodicals, there were 'Radio Fun' and 'Film Fun' featuring radio and film stars of that time but because they were printed entirely in black and white they held no appeal for me. A children's booklet by Enid Blyton called 'Sunny Stories' was published weekly, but most of us could not afford it on top of the others mentioned, but a girl in my class always had a copy and was prepared to lend it to selected classmates. She was never short of friends. When I got a little older I graduated to the *Hotspur* and the *Rover* comic books which were on sale on alternate weeks. They contained full length stories relating the adventures of a robot named 'Iron Man' in the first mentioned, and a cowboy called 'Solo Solomon' in the latter, both of them brave characters who were forever righting wrongs. Also featured were imaginative tales about unbeatable cricketers and, above all, an athlete named Wilson who developed unusual methods of training, running downhill with long strides, for example, until he could maintain those strides on the level thereby winning races streets ahead of his rivals. We never took these stories seriously but their entertainment value was immeasurable, and I still marvel how the authors managed to keep these series going week after week with a new twist to the themes I have mentioned.

After that I read all the adventure books I could find including *Robinson Crusoe*, *Treasure Island*, *The Coral Island*, and so on. My grandparents introduced me to the spirited antics of 'Just William' which, of course, I could relate to! By the age of twelve I was reading Guy de Maupassant stories and Edgar Allen Poe. I have always had a read in bed before going to sleep; after my mother came into my room to put out the light, at the appropriate time, I would get under the bedclothes and continue reading by torchlight. I believe it was this habit that ruined my eyesight and by the age of fourteen I needed glasses. However, my lust for reading stood me in good stead when, in later life, I joined the Merchant Navy and went to sea on ships where there was no entertainment whatsoever, and not even a wireless on my first one. As a result, most sailors were well-read and many of them obtained a high degree of self education because of it.

During and after the war years everyone depended on the wireless for news and entertainment. The main news was broadcast at 9 a.m., 1 p.m. and 9 p.m. as far as I remember. Priority was always for the latest developments in the fighting all over the world, not only against the Germans but the Japanese too, of course. These bulletins would sometimes be interspersed with extracts from Prime Minister Winston Churchill's latest speech which were stirring, patriotic and immensely inspiring. I had the privilege of hearing some of them live, including the 'we will never surrender' speech and his victory speech at the end of the war, rendered in his inimitable deep growl with 'Land of Hope and Glory' sounding gently in the background. My father was listening from the comfort of his armchair when suddenly he buried his head in his arms and broke down uncontrollably. Like so many thousands of servicemen, I have no doubt he was reminded of those he either knew or saw who never made it home. My sister Dilys and I had the good sense to go outside, leaving our dad to be comforted by our mother. The war crimes trials from Nuremburg were reported live and I vividly recall the last days when the Judges gave their verdicts to the former leaders of the Third Reich and sentenced them. My dad accurately predicted the fate of nearly every one of them.

In the daytime there was 'Housewives Choice' which, as the name implies, was a request programme for music of all kinds. 'Workers Playtime' was a similar one with comic items and loud applause from an audience, which may or may not have been those of factory workers somewhere. Often there would be a live concert by Glen Miller and his orchestra which unfailingly began with his famous piece 'In the Mood'. Other favourites that come to mind include 'Itma' with 'that man again – Tommy Handley' starring Mrs Mop with her introductory 'can I do you now Sir?' not forgetting the immortal Colonel Chinstrap whose cue was anything which might suggest a stiff drink. For example 'did you say double Sir? I don't mind if I do!' Wilfred Pickles, a bluff Yorkshire man, took his show all over Britain with his wife Mabel and a chap called Barney. He described the places they visited and interviewed interesting characters and handed them money prizes for answering simple questions. 'Give 'im the money Barney' was a catchphrase of the era. Wilfred came to Tavistock once and questioned a young man about life there and got a silly answer: 'I'd like to get a gun and walk around the town shooting into the air to wake everyone up'. I once came back from a long trip to sea and told my Uncle Syd, Tavistock was the same quiet place. 'You will be glad to come home one day Trevor' he said, and how right he was; but some of the changes I saw many years later appalled me.

To continue: Albert Sandler and his Palm Court Orchestra played classical pieces broadcast from Grand Hotel and was a favourite of my mother's. My mother and father argued about Grand Hotel every Sunday evening when the programme was broadcast; my father maintained the name Grand Hotel was just an invention but my mother insisted the music really was played at a hotel of that name and I believe she was later proved to be right. 'Family Favourites' was aired at lunch time on Sundays, yet another musical request programme where Cliff Michelmore began his illustrious career as a presenter. The immortal Gracie Fields and the 'Forces Sweetheart' Vera Lynn did wonders for the moral of ordinary people during the war years – they were British to the core and this was reflected in the songs they sang; 'Wish Me Luck as You Kiss Me Goodbye' by the former and 'White Cliffs of Dover' by our Vera were among the best known songs they sang. I have seen my mother run home from the shops after being told 'Our Gracie' was shortly to sing on the wireless.

Everybody I knew reserved a space for 6.45 p.m. weekdays, when 'Dick Barton, Special Agent' performed illustrious deeds for King and Country against foreign forces. He was helped by 'Jock' and 'Snowy' and there was nearly always a fight sequence with grunts and gasps as blows were audibly exchanged but, of course, our hero won every time. My favourite broadcaster was Valentine Dyall ('The Man in Black') who narrated the horror stories of Maupassant and Poe in a tone of voice that thrilled, and at the same time, frightened his listeners who nevertheless felt compelled to hear him out. His half hour programme started at 4.30 p.m. and I used to run home from school so as not to miss a word of it.

Radio Luxembourg's non-stop popular music programmes caught the imagination of every young person in the country. The BBC refused to follow suit for several years in the face of growing competition, not only from the continent but from what was referred to as a 'Pirate Radio' ship anchored, I believe, at the mouth of the River Thames. There was only the BBC in those days and they had government backing who quickly saw to it the 'pirates' were outlawed and shut down. Not long afterwards 'pop' music became a feature of the BBC, and when television became established 'Top of the Pops' was to be one of the most successful and long running programmes ever.

Every sporting event was covered, of course, and boxing matches in particular attracted wide audiences. I listened to the fearsome scraps the late Freddie Mills had (he took some cruel beatings and later took his own life). Bruce Woodcock's momentous heavyweight fight with the American Jo Baksi was a classic in bravery. Woodcock suffered a broken jaw in one of the early rounds and fought on for several more, taking a terrible hammering before the referee stopped the bout, from which Bruce never fully recovered. He was Britain's hero and whenever his boxing match ended he always said a few words to sum up the contest, ending every time with 'Hello Mum – I'm OK and will be home in five hours' (he was from Yorkshire and lived with his mother). Boxing commentaries were nearly always by a man whose surname was Andrews, supported by inter-round summing up by W. Barrington-Dalby. Andrews had an American style manner (he was Canadian I think) and fired off phrases like 'that was a beautiful right hook which nearly sent ____ out of the living room through the kitchen and into the backyard' and similar comments. As for Barrington-Dalby many of us regarded him as a sadist, a typical comment from him being something like '____ landed a crushing blow right under the heart and sent his opponent staggering against the ropes, but he's a good strong boy and isn't finished yet'.

Cricket commentaries lasted all day and every ball bowled was described and analysed. Heroes of the day, among many others, were Dennis Compton, a very stylish batsman who was a treat to watch. I once saw him play at Lords when he scored heavily and acknowledged his fifty by simply raising his bat to acknowledge the applause – there were none of the childish antics seen today like 'punching the air' for example; Bill Edrich, a hard hitter at the crease who once hit a ball clean out of the ground; the Bedser twins, Eric and Alec, both bowlers of repute, and there was no arguing with the Umpire or smacking of palms with their team-mates because they'd taken a wicket; and Freddie Evans, a Welshman who played wicket keeper for England for many years; indeed, the team would not have been complete without him. All of them were outstanding sportsmen in the truest sense.

Footballers enjoyed the same adulation but not the fabulous salaries they get these days. Stanley Matthews and Stanley Mortensen are two players that live on in memory. I don't believe either of them were ever involved in foul play or 'booked' by the referee. Plymouth Argyle was widely supported and buses took men and boys (I do not remember any female fans on any of the buses) to Home Park from Tavistock and most of the surrounding villages. The driver/owner was a Mr Goodman who drove the Tavistock bus and picked up his customers in Bedford Square. His premises lay on the right hand side of the road leading from Drakes Statue to the mini-roundabout in Ford Street where he also sold petrol. Argyle's football stadium was very basic at that time, resembling a bomb site. Standing only was the rule for most fans on rough ground and there were no safety barriers. Regular supporters took a small wooden box to stand on so they could see over the heads of those in front. A regular feature was someone in the crowd who played bugle calls for each eventuality – 'Last Post' for injury or a goal scored against the home team and 'Reveille' when a hurt player got up and renewed playing. Whoever it was, ex-army or a Royal Marine perhaps, he was a fervent supporter who followed Argyle everywhere and boy could he play a bugle – perfect notes every time. As for the players, there was no spitting or snarling and I do not recall hearing any foul language. The team had a run of bad results just after the war and the state of the pitch or a shower of rain was often referred to as partly to blame, giving rise to a well-known refrain which went like this:

'Owing to the wind and rain,
Poor old Argyle lost again'.

Except for the compulsory games played at school I have neither had the time nor the inclination to actively pursue or watch sporting events, neither was I a talented player which is why my memories of the various sports activities in my home town are scanty. This is not a history book but an account of life as I remember it and therefore my remarks are necessarily brief. Tavistock Football Club ground used to be at the top of Green Lane on the left as the road levels off. Shortly after the end of the Second World War, Pitts Cleave Quarry owner Mr Langsford gave the land at Crowndale, where the ground now is, to the club and it is named Langsford Park after him (the Green Lane field was then allocated to Dolvin Road School). Cricket then, as now, was a regular event at The Ring on Whitchurch Down, certainly one of the most spectacular venues in Britain. Likewise Tavistock Golf Club embraces a course whose vast panoramic views are equal to any other. The tennis and bowling club facilities in Plymouth Road were always well supported.

For the majority of townsfolk, the main source of entertainment was the cinema. I saw the Carlton cinema, which stood on the corner of Russell Street and Plymouth Road, being built just before the start of the Second World War, on my way to and from the Council School in Plymouth Road. When it first opened I recall a tall, grey haired, elegant man who held the grand title of 'Commissionaire'. He wore a green cap with a gold braided peak and was dressed in a long, military style, dark green coat with two vertical rows of large brass buttons and huge cuffs with gold braid. He paraded up and down outside with a winning smile, announcing in a gruff voice the vacant seats and the prices thereof to the queues waiting for admission, often in the rain. The Yanks, as we called them, always collared the best seats with their girl friends and the atmosphere was often a pale shade of blue with cigarette and pipe smoke. I have witnessed a pipe smoker lighting up during the performance and seeing great clouds of smoke spiralling upwards and temporarily obliterating much of the screen. In the post war years there was a customary interval when pretty young girls would parade up the aisles with illuminated trays, with perhaps ices, chocolate bars and soft drinks for sale.

There were always queues during the war years, with a colourful sprinkling of uniforms worn by our own boys and the Americans. The cinemas were always packed, and in the 'old cinema' waiting customers often opted for 'standing room only' which entailed standing at the back or on the side of the auditorium until a seat became vacant. The term 'side' meant standing on the steps leading to the emergency exits and, as far as I know, they are still there inside the present shop. Incidentally, usherettes with torches were on hand to conduct patrons to their seats and there was a constant coming and going by people who had either been admitted from the lengthy queues after the start of the film, or were leaving when the story reached the 'this is where we came in' point to be replaced by yet more customers who had been waiting patiently outside. There were rarely any empty seats in either of the two cinemas.

The word 'movies' was unknown then, by the way, and was first heard when the American soldiers came to Tavistock – even then it was to be many years before it was widely adopted. We went to the 'pictures' or, as we sometimes called it, 'the flicks'. The latter term evolved as a result of the dubious quality of some of the films we saw from an earlier time and anyone who has seen an old silent film will know exactly what I mean. Until 1939, nearly every picture was in black and white and I remember the first Technicolor films shown in Tavistock, for which there was an increase in the admission charge.

The films we saw are related in the chapter 'Boyhood Days Part 2' but we could only get admission for those films allocated a 'U' Certificate by the British Board of Censors. This indicated it was suitable viewing for all ages whereas an 'A' film was considered the sort of entertainment where a child under sixteen had to be accompanied by an adult. The result was that we congregated outside the cinemas and subjected ourselves to the moral dangers of asking strange men or women to 'please take us in' which they mostly did, but nevertheless abandoned us once inside. I recall going to see every boy's ultimate adventure film *Buffalo Bill* and being refused admission because it was 'A' category. Another ridiculous 'A' category was slapped on the Errol Flynn version of *Robin Hood*. Nearly every film I remember seeing, whether alone or accompanied by an adult has since been shown on television without restraint and to me the most shocking scenes are commonplace these days prefixed by the meaningless 'PG' symbol (Parental Guidance advised). Swearing, even of the mildest nature in any film, was simply not permitted but there were two exceptions worth relating. The final words spoken by Clark Gable in 'Gone with the Wind' were 'frankly my dear I don't give a damn'. Ordinarily the word 'damn' would have been deleted but because the spoken emphasis was on 'give' and not 'damn' it was overlooked. In 'Scott of the Antarctic' Petty Officer Evans is depicted telling a joke about a Gunnery Officer berating his class about the number of men losing a thumb tip during gunnery practice. He went through the motions of loading the gun in question and with a look of pained surprise when finished said '...and that's how you lose the tip of your bloody thumb!' There was an audible gasp from the cinema audience, not of shock but surprise that such a thing had been said on the screen. Today, when I hear the very worst of curses and obscenities uttered daily on television, I sometimes think the world really has been turned upside down.

'X' rated films were for people over the age of twenty-one I believe.

After the wireless bulletins and the newspapers our news was graphically illustrated in the 'British Movietone' and 'Pathe News', always featured at the cinemas between the main film and the so-called 'B' picture or serial that followed. They gave us a visual report of the news we had probably heard or read about already. We boys revelled in the battle scenes from the war zones but were shocked like everyone else when the horrific images of the concentration camps, the gas chambers and the piles of skeletal dead bodies that were revealed (no film censor 'A' category was applied for these sequences by the way). All the above activities were to be enjoyed by adults and children alike but for young children, and those we refer to as 'teenagers' nowadays, there were other things to hand as described in Part 2.

Leisure (Part 2)

Of all the official acts of vandalism that have taken place in my home town some of the worst have been perpetrated on our lovely Meadows. What happened to the paddling pool for instance? This beautiful spot was a favourite with many families with children when I was a boy, either splashing in the water or sailing our toy boats, mainly little yachts. A large round shallow pool (see photo) was flanked by a smaller square pool on either side with sand pits at the western end where toddlers were safe to play. It was paradise for us kids where we could indulge in all sorts of fun, quite safely, under the watchful eye of our mothers who gathered in a secluded semi-circular alcove with wooden seats, sheltered from the wind by a short trimmed laurel hedge. There they could observe us at all times whilst engaging in the latest gossip. There was an overflow from the Tavistock canal which flowed continuously into the pool, and an overflow from the pool to the river Tavy at a lower level, thus ensuring a clean water supply at all times. In winter the pool was drained and left dry until the spring. What happy memories I have of sunny afternoons in summertime, when literally dozens of children shouted and laughed together in perfect safety – something the children of today are missing for no reason at all.

The Paddling Pool in the Meadows. What happy times were had by generations of Tavistock children. It and the Lily Pond are no more. (Courtesy of Tavistock History Society)

The Lily Pond. The children are probably looking for newts as I and my friends used to do. (Courtesy Tavistock History Society)

There was also a very attractive lily pond upon which floated the large green leaves and flowers of that aquatic plant. Like the paddling pool it was edged with smooth, round-edged slabs which overhung the water slightly and under which numbers of newts were to be found. We boys used to spend hours on our bellies searching for the newts who shared the pond with a number of goldfish; the tiny dragon-like creatures fascinated us and were quite harmless. In the centre of the pond was a dark brown square pillar roughly six foot high, from which a fountain spouted on hot sunny days creating an enchanting spectacle. That too has disappeared and there is no trace today of the pond. And what about the swings and the see-saw? As I recall, there were two sets of swings, three for older children and another set of three tiny ones with a safety bar for toddlers. Beside the see-saw was a mini-roundabout. Every passing mum paused to allow their children the simple pleasures enjoyed by generations of Tavistock boys and girls – but no more, because for some reason they have been removed. Will it be the turn of the bandstand next I wonder?

Then again, at the Westbridge end of the meadows there used to be goal posts where boys could play football in a realistic manner and a large shelter where they, and any spectators, could go if it rained. Now they too are gone, together with another shelter at the town end, the adjacent swings etc. described above and the two wartime Nissen huts, which I must admit were not in keeping with the otherwise idyllic surroundings. Meadowlands now occupies the site and I have no argument with that.

As for leisure hours spent indoors, my home always seemed to resound with music. My mother was a very able pianist and the upright piano we possessed was in constant use, especially during those war years when my father was absent. Very often my mother would sit and play from memory for perhaps an hour, delivering selections from the popular musicals of the pre-war era. I feel it must have helped her deal with the loneliness she had to endure. Sometimes our neighbour Mr Reed, who was a talented pianist and played the organ at the Abbey Chapel, would join in. His piano was situated against the dividing wall between our flat and his and could be clearly heard, as were his comments such as 'shall we do (naming a piece of music) together Mrs James?' to which I have heard my mother reply 'Yes! You start us off Mr Reed' and so he would, with my mother following and the two pianos blended in harmony. I have never forgotten those performances. My father could sing. He possessed a deep baritone voice and often he and my mother would suddenly decide to have a musical evening or afternoon recital when he sang those classic songs 'Yeomen of England', 'Glorious Devon', Floral Dance', and his favourite 'Little Grey Home in the West', among many others. For my father these interludes were often rehearsals for performing at concerts in Tavistock Town Hall with Mr R. Bawden, a bass singer of renown in the district. The neighbours never complained – indeed, I was often stopped by one of them who would tell me how much she enjoyed listening to them.

My parents were fond of walking and most Sundays, on the rare occasions my father was home, we would set off on at least a six mile hike, often through Crowndale Woods along the canal towpath or to Harford Bridge via Nutley Lane and back along the main road to Parkwood. I was not always keen to go walking and when I was very young I would complain my legs were aching, expecting to get carried a short distance or stop for a rest. No such luck! 'It's because the walk is doing you good' I was told and there is some truth in that. Opposite the entrance to College Avenue was the GWR railway embankment (previously mentioned), which had an archway under it leading to a small farm, in front of which was a long green field that stretched all the way to where Kelly College playing field car park now is. One sunny day we had a picnic by the River Tavy at a spot below Evans' Weir, when a highly irate man ran towards us bellowing for us to get off his land and waving a stick. It frightened my mother but my dad was on survivor leave after his ship was sunk in the Arctic and did not scare easily. We paused until the angry landowner arrived and confronted my father, muttering bloodcurdling threats as to what might happen if we delayed our departure. My father asked him who he was and who he thought he was talking to. 'Don't you know who I am? I'm Colonel F_____' he roared red faced and shaking with rage. 'I don't care if you're the King of Turkey' was the answer he got 'and if you wave that stick at me again I will take it from you and throw it in the river and you after it. We are just leaving anyway'. Our aggressor was speechless and we left with 'colours flying'.

When my dad was away, there were regular family picnics when my aunts and cousins would join forces and pack sandwiches and a primus with which to boil a kettle for tea, and tramp many miles to our favourite picnic venues. Pew Tor and Peter Tavy Cleave were often visited. We boys grew up fit and strong with a love of wild, lonely places, and in adult life I have walked alone in all kinds of weather all over Dartmoor, often setting off before dawn to reach my favourite tor or coombe that was to be a starting point for my trek by sunrise. I have inherited my mother's love of the moors. When young, she would often rise early on a Sunday and walk many miles to a picturesque spot where there is a stone cross (these were guideposts in medieval times) and be home again

Pixies Cross on Whitchurch Down looking towards Dartmoor proper. (Author's collection)

before her parents were up – and they were early risers. Pixies Cross on Whitchurch Down was one of her favourite destinations and she once confided to me that she and two close friends unfailingly walked there early each May Day and daubed their faces in the dew, in the belief it worked a charm that would ensure a handsome lover would come for them one fine day. They didn't believe it but performed the ritual just in case – ancient traditions die hard!

Organised activities were necessarily limited until the war ended and were confined mainly to the cubs and scout movements. I joined the cubs when I was at Council School when our 'Akala' (pack leader) was one of our teachers, Miss Moon. To be honest, although she did her best and I'm sure she served our little group well, for me it was not exciting enough compared to my other boyhood deeds. I did not remain a member for long and quietly left. I think Miss Moon was disappointed in me and with some justification. When I was a little older, and during the last year of the war, I joined the scouts; they had their 'den' beneath the council offices in Drake Road. This was more like it I thought, learning to tie knots, rambling over the downs, and enjoying the occasional camp fires when we cooked and ate sausages impaled on short sticks held over the glowing embers. On one occasion we joined forces with other scouts and had a giant camp fire in the meadows, where we sat singing the favourite scouting songs of those times 'Shenandoah', 'Ten Green Bottles', 'Polly Wolly Doodle' and others. I suppose it was rather juvenile by the standards of today but for us it was a wonderful exercise in camaraderie and forming firm friendships.

The highlight of my scouting was boxing. We Tavistock boys were very fortunate in having the services (freely given) of two Royal Marine Commandos from Bickleigh camp, who I believe were physical training instructors. Every 'scout night' they would pair us off with lads of similar build and drill us in the time honoured classical style of boxing – straight lefts, right cross counters, uppercuts etc. It gave us huge confidence and no-one was seriously hurt, after all a bleeding nose or a bruise or two never really mattered to us. We were thrilled to be learning a skill that would stand us in good stead for the rest of our lives (here I might add that professional boxing is quite another matter and does not have my support). Then came the day when we would be tested in earnest. A boxing tournament was arranged one Saturday night in the Pannier Market between us and the Bere Alston scouts. A full size ring was erected and seating provided for the public who supported us handsomely. I cannot remember how many bouts there were or indeed who won but I do recall my own contest. Our Royal Marine friends were in our corner giving us advice and in my case it was 'he's wide open to an uppercut lad – give it to him and see him off!' Well, I gave it to him in fine style and 'saw him off' but in the process I hit him with the inside of my glove and broke my thumb. My right hand swelled and turned blue all over and yes, it hurt like hell, but after seeing a doctor who wrapped it firmly in plaster I was quite a celebrity for some weeks afterwards.

While I was still at school a gentleman called Don Connett did much for the young people in Tavistock. The son of a former Tavistock policeman, Don as he always liked to be called, held the position of Magistrates Clerk and was universally respected as a man of integrity. He and some colleagues whom I have no knowledge of formed the 'Wescon Club' based in a single storey building half-way up Kilworthy Hill on the right. The place was full on club nights when there was (recorded) music, soft drinks, table tennis and a small billiards table. Most of all it was somewhere for girls and boys to get together in the nicest way.

One day, my friend John Greening took me to the Liberal Club in West Street. The club, which was non-political, occupied the first floor above the 'old cinema' and comprised a large room with two full sized billiard tables and another room with table tennis table and bats. I was an accomplished table tennis player then (at thirteen years of age) but had never seen a billiard table and had no knowledge of that game or of snooker either. The man in charge was an unforgettable character called Joe Bowhay (always addressed by us boys as Mister Bowhay), a middle aged man then who was short in stature but who commanded a great deal of respect from everyone who knew him. He was a former quarry worker who lost his right arm and leg in an accident where a railway truck ran over him when he fell after losing his balance on slippery rail sleepers. It was a lesson in bravery and sheer determination to watch this man tie his shoelaces and knot his tie with the one left hand he had and don his overcoat single-handed.

He approached me in the traditional Devonshire manner to politely ask my name and where I lived. Further conversational probing revealed my mother's family name (Doidge), when he at once recognised my Uncle Syd and my Uncle Charlie and I was welcomed into the fold. John showed me how to hold a cue and create a bridge for it by tucking my thumb upwards and spreading my fingers wide for support and, after several more visits, we both became promising players. Often we would be lining up to take our shot when Mr Bowhay would appear behind us, saying for example, 'are you going to try and go in – off the red? Well you need some left hand side – not too much mind – and hit the cue ball about here' indicating with his finger where he meant. Sure enough, all went just as he forecast nearly every time. Sometimes he would have a game; he used a wooden block with grooves cut into the sides at various angles as a rest for his cue and showed us that despite his handicap he was not a man to be trifled with on the billiard table. Of course, we played snooker too and a game called 'Life' where four or five players each had a different coloured ball, and when it was your turn you tried to pot one of your opponent's balls whilst leaving your own safe. The last man left 'alive' won and as a rule won a small sum of money – the proceeds of bets furtively made beforehand.

Then there were nights when visiting teams came to compete with our own picked team. I have often watched Mr Bowhay preparing the tables during the afternoon prior to competition night. The tables were first brushed, always in one direction only from the baulk end, and it was surprising how much debris was collected as a result. Then came the ironing, again all in one direction, with a huge flat iron that must have taxed that man's strength as he swung it onto the table and proceeded with his one left arm to iron the cloth (again in one direction only) the full length of the table. This operation was carried out without stopping and in parallel swathes as far as the middle of the table, then he would complete the job on the opposite side. By 4 o'clock all was ready and the covers were laid. One of the most outstanding players (and I cannot recall who he played for) was an elegant gentleman called Moncrief, and on competition night the viewing area overlooking the table he was on would be crowded. He was 'upper class' both in appearance and ability, and my brother-in-law Ron Marks recently told me how much he owed to Mr Moncrief who he played against on numerous occasions and from whom, by observation, he learned so much. It stood him in good stead later when he (Ron) became Billiards Champion of Devon and Cornwall.

A day to remember was when a coach trip was organized for us to see the great Joe Davis, for twenty years undefeated World Snooker Champion, at Okehampton market hall. What an experience that was! We watched entranced by his every move, as he demonstrated what to us were impossible shots, and played a few frames with local club players before showing off some even more impossible trick shots. For us boys it was an unforgettable experience and for weeks afterwards we all tried to emulate some of his skills and learned a lot in the process.

In retrospect I realise just how much we young lads owed to the club and to Joe Bowhay in particular. We always had somewhere we could go and be welcome on dull wet days and some sunny ones too. I strongly feel we need more men of his calibre today than ever before as his presence at all times created a homely atmosphere instead of the cold, lifeless, dull environment of empty premises. As far as I know there was never a 'bad egg in the basket' and that in my view was entirely due to this man – a 'fatherly figure'.

Christmases were austere events by today's standards but I truly feel there was a great deal more sincerity and meaning during those war years. We did not enjoy the glut of Christmas cards, decorations, balloons, Christmas trees, paper hats, coloured lights, or food items we take for granted now. Schoolchildren made paper chains in class by cutting sheets of coloured paper into strips and gluing the ends to form interlocking loops of different colours in sufficient numbers to form a chain, and that was about all the decorations there were apart from some holly perhaps. There were I believe some little extras allowed in our rations – dried fruit, for example, for puddings but the treats were few and a chicken for dinner that day was the norm. I personally never had turkey until I went to sea. My recollections of Christmas Day are of family gatherings in my Aunt Mary's house in Brook Street where the adults cheered one another up with hopeful predictions about how the war might be over by next year. I once heard my Uncle Syd reassuring my mother about how my dad could only be involved in 'mopping up' operations when we all knew he was in Sicily or Italy (he was seconded from the Royal Navy to the Eighth Army) and in the thick of the fighting. We children were entertained by simple games like 'I Spy' or 'Find the Thimble' which entailed a thimble being placed in some unlikely location in the room but visible at all times. It was surprising how easily the seekers could be deceived: for example, on one occasion someone simply placed it on his head and the search for it lasted a record time!

My mother would play the piano for a family sing-song when our favourite carols would be sung (all from memory) and then a selection of old time music hall items with solo renderings by the bravest among us. One of them was my aunt's next door neighbour 'Johnny' Waterfield. He possessed a splendid tenor voice and always sang for us, the pure high notes resounding outside to the delight of passers-by. He was born in a humble home in Paul's Almshouses (mentioned elsewhere in this narrative) and my mother recalled him literally singing for his supper in Bedford Square on Saturday nights and being grateful for the pennies he received. Under happier circumstances there can be no doubt he could have made a comfortable living with his musical abilities.

Did Father Christmas manage to make his traditional visits on Christmas Eve? Yes he did, and despite the wartime shortages the gifts he brought sometimes surprised all of us when we woke at some unearthly hour of the morning to examine the good things he left. At around seven or eight years of age the inevitable doubts entered our heads as to whether or not the great benefactor was real. These suspicions were fuelled by hints and quiet rumours circulated by some of our more sophisticated classmates and I for one hung up my stocking with much scepticism one year but when I saw the good things left for me, things I knew my parents could never have afforded (!!!) all misgivings vanished in my exclamation about 'what a dear old man he (Father Christmas) was'.

One item that was missing was the profusion of drink that typifies the festive season these days. There was very little consumption of alcoholic drinks in the home; men did their drinking in the pubs. In the first place it simply wasn't available and it was not uncommon for beer stocks to run out in the pubs on busy nights. Spirits were rationed and rarely seen at home; a few bottles of brown ale sold over the counter by obliging landlords were often all there was to be had. Wine was consumed only by 'toffs' or in posh restaurants. I remember an aunt telling me how my cousin had been promoted to manager in the jewellery business where he worked and that his boss had taken him out for dinner where they had 'wine and everything'. It duly impressed me as it was meant to do. I and most people I knew prophesied wine drinking would never catch on in this country when it was first introduced on a mass scale many years later. The British only want their beer, we said. Just how wrong can you be?

Birthday parties for children were very modest affairs by comparison with those of today. There were no paper hats, balloons, fancy dress outfits or entertainers present and generally the number of guests was limited to two or three 'best' friends – the rationing would not permit catering for larger gatherings. The mothers must have saved and scrimped for weeks to give their visitors treats like jelly, for example, or fruit cake for tea. Presents were simple items, mainly books and occasionally small sums of money. We played indoor games on these occasions. Musical chairs was a favourite as was 'pass the parcel', and we had just as much fun and enjoyment in our own way as youngsters of today, gathering in a church hall and being entertained by a conjurer, for example, and being given a token present each. I once went to a friend's birthday tea and had rabbit pie. He lived in a poor area of the town and his parents had little or nothing else to offer but gave us what they had with a good heart. The recipients thought nothing of it as it was wartime, and in any case we were happy to be together with our pal in a happy home – which it was.

My final comment on our leisure time is to say we often had hilarious times. I and my generation as a whole harbour no jealousy or envy or disapproval concerning children's pleasures today. I can remember the thrill of being taken to see a full-length Walt Disney film when the latest technology was employed to make it possible. The fabulous graphics that go into the production of *Harry Potter* films or *Lord of the Rings* are wonderful accomplishments to us older ones, but I fear that for young people they are just another phase in a world where, as I have said elsewhere, nothing is impossible. As for the cartoon type films that we talked about for days after seeing them, television producers have made them so commonplace they are not only taken for granted but fail to give that surge of pleasure I recall from all those years ago. Nevertheless, when I observe three thousand or more young people taking part in the gruelling Ten Tors challenge on Dartmoor every year my heart warms to them and I only wish the same opportunities had been open to me and my friends – we would have jumped at the chance to do the same. Whatever some may say I am of the opinion these are the good times for young and old alike, and with the knowledge and confidence gained early in life by so many young men and women now, surely we are at least seeing the beginnings of a better world.

Transport

Almost everyone I knew as a boy relied on public transport to go places. A special shopping trip or visit to the theatre was only possible in Plymouth and, immediately after the war, shopping in particular was limited as a result of the blitz. Plymouth took a terrible pounding from German bombers and although the target was the dockyard the centre of the town was devastated and most of the big stores with it. Nevertheless temporary shops soon sprang up amongst the ruins and the good old Palace Theatre which had escaped any damage whatsoever provided first class entertainment all year round. A day in Plymouth was a treat.

As already mentioned in this book there were two railway connections from Tavistock to Plymouth. One was the GWR single track line via Horrabridge, Yelverton, Bickleigh, and Laira to Millbay. The 'Southern Railway' as it was always known was a double track main line that connected Plymouth to Waterloo station in London. This line from Tavistock to Plymouth was via Bere Alston, Bere Ferrers, Tamerton Foliot, St. Budeaux, Devonport and Plymouth North Road. The latter was the most used because it was more central to the town centre. The GWR main line to Plymouth from London was via Torbay and thence over the Saltash Bridge to Penzance. Their 'Cornish Riviera Express' took this route and was famous nationwide. The 'Southern' introduced a rival service shortly after the war with the 'Devon Belle' which boasted Pullman coaches throughout and an 'Observation Car' at the rear of the train. The same company built the streamlined West Country Class engines all of which were named after towns in that area. There was one called 'Tavistock' (see picture on page 142) and the entire senior section of the Grammar School (including the author) marched to the station one afternoon and boarded the footplate one at a time.

Trains then always came and were always on time – it would have been unthinkable and unforgivable for one to be cancelled or even delayed by a shortage of drivers, for example. You could buy a ticket at any station where there was a ticket office to any other station in Britain at a fixed fare. The passenger coaches were generally clean and free of litter unless you caught the 'workman's train' mainly for dockyard workers, leaving Tavistock at an early hour and returning late afternoon. Manual workers in those days did not have the benefit of locker rooms or adequate washing facilities like showers, and so they travelled to and fro' in their working clothes and this was reflected in the grubby state of the carriage they occupied – usually the one immediately behind the engine. Wartime train journeys were a nightmare as services were restricted anyway and priority given to troop movements. I have seen railway stations (and trains) packed to overflowing with soldiers on the move and have stood with my parents in the corridors of the old fashioned trains for hours. How the

West Country Class steam engine 'Tavistock'. (Courtesy of the National Railway Museum, York and the Science and Social Picture Library, London)

soldiers managed to cram onto and off trains with the kitbags, packs and rifles they all carried I will never know.

Some of the branch line journeys were a delight and, in particular, I have in mind the quaint little train that connected Yelverton to Princetown on Dartmoor. It was jokingly referred to either as the 'Princetown Flyer' or the 'Convict Express' in earlier times when Dartmoor Prison inmates were transferred to and from Dartmoor by train. Princetown lies 1400 foot above sea level and therefore the line was an uphill gradient nearly all the way, with hairpin bends around some of the tors. It was a small train as a rule, with just two carriages, but I have travelled on it when there were more than that with a couple of goods trucks as well, and actually witnessed the engine going past in the opposite direction on one particular bend. The line closed in 1956 when the 'Beeching Axe' fell on so many branch lines (and some main ones too) but there can be no doubt if it was operating today it would be among the biggest attractions in the west.

The bus services were exclusively 'Western National' who provided 'double-decker' buses for long journeys, to Plymouth or Launceston or Okehampton, and single-deckers to Whitchurch, Princetown, and other outlying places. The double-deckers always carried a Conductor, the majority of whom were women during the war years and immediately afterwards, who took the fares during the journey and gave change from a large leather bag they wore. They also issued tickets from a metal dispenser

'The Convict Express' or 'Princetown Flier' approaching Princetown. This was a branch line from Yelverton to Princetown operated by the GWR. (Painting by Paul Deacon)

that pinged as the ticket emerged and was 'punched'. One feature of all buses, which will surprise the modern reader, were the small rectangular metal plates with a ridged criss-cross pattern fixed to the back of every seat and known as 'stubbers', the purpose of which was for smokers to safely stub out their cigarette ends. At intervals along the top and lower decks were push buttons which passengers pressed once to ring a bell or buzzer to indicate to the driver they wanted to get off at the next stop. Unlike most of these types of buses now, the driver was isolated in a separate cab at the front and the passenger access on and off was from a platform at the rear. After leaving the vehicle the conductor, who was stationed on the platform by the stairway, judged when it was safe to pull away and pressed the bell button twice to signal the driver to proceed.

There was no bus station in Tavistock only a 'Western National' office in Bedford Square under the central arch beneath the Town Hall where the Information Centre now is. All buses terminated at and departed from Bedford Square and their arrival and departure times were monitored by an Inspector who often boarded the buses for part of the journey and checked passenger's tickets. The long distance buses, to Plymouth for example, were restricted to one every hour during and after the end of the war and consequently they were filled to capacity with as many as eight or nine people standing along the lower deck. I remember conductors calling out 'one more standing!' just before departure and often passengers already on board would be

Town Hall and Bedford Square. Note the bus parked at what used to be the terminus for all buses (there was no bus station). A taxi is seen parked on the rank (right) in front of the church. (Courtesy of Tavistock History Society)

asked to get off if their destination was Westbridge, for instance, to make room for those going to Plymouth.

Like the trains the bus services were reliable and punctual; essential in an age where few cars were to be seen and large numbers of workers and some servicemen commuted daily to Plymouth. When I observe the clogged thoroughfares at rush hour times nowadays, I seriously believe things could be better by re-introducing (with some improvements it must be said) the transport system we used to have.

I Go Out Into the World

When I left school two months before my sixteenth birthday, my life became empty. I had made no plans and had no ambitions. My one and only dream had been to join the Royal Marines Band Service. In those days they recruited youngsters at fourteen and a half as Boy Buglers, and as soon as I reached that age I applied and went for interview in Devonport. I passed the education and physical examination without trouble but the last test was for eyesight and I failed. It was the biggest disappointment of my life, and even now when I see those magnificent musicians on parade I think to myself that is still the only real ambition I ever had and it was denied me.

A kindly neighbour who was the chief baker at the Co-operative bakery in Market Street put a word in and got me a job working with him. It entailed a 4 a.m. start, timed for me to assist drawing the first batch of bread from the huge ovens and then greasing 500 bread tins by hand for the next batch. After that I did cleaning work and assisted generally until the last batch of bread was taken out. One of my more pleasant tasks was taking doughnuts out of the fryer and dusting them with fine sugar and, needless to say, not all of them made it to the receptacle they were meant for! One other job comes to mind. The bakery also made small currant buns and one day there was an oversight and some were slightly burnt. I was given two huge open topped tins, one of jam and the other with coconut. I had to sort and remove the burnt currant buns which were then dipped into the jam and then coated with sugar to disguise their condition. They were sold for a penny extra! It was a very happy place of work. Mr Bond, the neighbour who helped me, was a chorister in the Parish Church and two other men, one of whom was called Tucker, were Salvationists. For most of each shift they sang hymns, harmonising 'barber shop' style and I too sang with them. I was the only one who required mittens for handling the newly-baked bread (believe me it was hot) to the amusement of my colleagues who did it all with bare hands. I suppose after years of such work their hands were devoid of sensitivity.

Then I was sent to work in the dairy. Milk was sold in glass bottles in those days in pints and half-pints and hundreds of them had to be washed and sterilised in big metal tubs with two motor driven revolving brushes on top designed to fit the inside of the bottles. My job was taking the badly stained ones and holding them over the brushes until they were clean. Then the production line was started where a conveyor belt fed the bottles onto a circular section beneath an overhead tank with injectors that fitted over each bottle in turn. In one revolution each bottle was filled and passed along another conveyor to where I was waiting with an enormous cardboard box full of silvery metal tops which I placed on every bottle before it passed to a 'press' which came briefly down and sealed the edges. You would be surprised how tiring this job could be and a loss of concentration meant bottles passing through without a top and you would be a very unpopular man.

One day I noticed there was a vacancy for a Trainee Reporter on the *Tavistock Times* which was one of two local newspapers, the other being the *Tavistock Gazette*. It appealed to me at once and I duly submitted an application together with a sample of my writing from my schooldays. I got the job and was privileged to work under the guidance of one of the kindest and most generous bosses I ever worked for – the late Mr E. Whitaker. He was a bluff Yorkshire man who owned and edited the paper. His background was a saga that included selling newspapers on the streets of Keighley at eleven years of age; commissioned from the ranks in the trenches during the First World War ('you always knew when we were about to be attacked' he used to say 'the rats left the trenches in droves'); crime reporter for a national newspaper (all the 'nationals' occupied premises in Fleet Street in London then); managing a German circus towards the end of the Second World War to entertain Allied soldiers; then returning to journalism and becoming owner/editor of a newspaper in Scotland before taking to the road selling books from a 'camper van' which is how he first came to Tavistock.

What a man he was; bursting with energy and full of ideas. One of the first things he did when he took over the *Tavistock Times* was to form the 'Sunshine Circle' which children of all ages could join. New entrants had the thrill of being allocated a membership number which, together with their names, were published in a special column set aside for them. Hundreds of elderly men and women living in Tavistock today will recall 'Uncle Jon' and the outings he organised from time to time. I accompanied them once on a coach trip to Paignton with the irrepressible Mr Whitaker, laughing and joking with us all the way there and back. He was a talented ventriloquist and brought a 'dummy' figure with him to entertain us with and the kids loved it. When we got onto the beach he was the first to don a swimming costume and run into the sea. For a man in his sixties he really was remarkable.

I was not yet 16 when I began a life of unrivalled variety. Every morning I would visit the police station and the ambulance depot to see if anything of note had occurred. Each week there would be a Magistrates Court held in the Guildhall under the Chairmanship of Mr R. Morsehead where I saw and heard things I never imagined. In the main, the cases heard related to theft, domestic violence (one sensational such case involved the use of a gun), car offences, and fraud. A local taxi driver was a regular 'customer', usually on a charge of speeding and occasional dangerous driving. The same man would always turn out for me in later life when I came home on leave from the Merchant Navy late at night. He would drive me to my home in Brentor in his dressing gown and slippers and be back home in bed 'before he woke up properly' as he used to say with a grin. I often marvelled at the eloquence displayed by defendant's legal representatives and learned a lot from them. Often I would cringe in sympathy with certain individuals appearing on some relatively minor charge when the prosecuting solicitor slammed into witnesses relentlessly; but then the defendant's solicitor would rise and utterly demolish their evidence. It was an education for me but I was not permitted to attend the court when a man I knew was being tried for a sexual assault on a child. 'You are not going' said Mr Whitaker to me, 'you would be shocked' and of course, he was right.

The several concerts, amateur dramatics, the annual Hunt Ball, etc. held in the Town Hall were all attended by me, and a full report with as many people named as possible was the norm. Early in my new career I went to a concert in a village near Tavistock given by the local W.I. In my innocence I wrote just what I thought about it, all of it

The *Tavistock Times* offices as they appear today – outwardly unchanged since my time there. (Author's photo)

truthful. Mr Whitaker called me to one side when he read it, saying 'was it really that bad?' and when I answered, 'yes it was' his response was 'well, let them down gently Laddie' and proceeded to change my account to a more acceptable style with phrases like 'pleasant rendering', 'charming piece' etc. I have never forgotten that lesson. At other times he could be brutal in his criticism. 'No, no, Laddie – this won't do' he would say, while wielding a large cartoon type blue pencil and crossing out my offering, but at the same time giving advice as to what the right approach should be. 'In years to come you may say to yourself old man Whitaker was a hard man but by golly I wish he'd been harder!' he once remarked. All I can say is I am grateful for everything he taught me and always will be. Any literary success I may have is entirely due to his encouragement and interest in me.

TAVISTOCK'S 'UNCLE JON' DIES, AGED 85

MR ERNEST WHITAKER, known affectionately to many thousands of Tavistock people as "Uncle Jon," from the title of a children's corner in the local newspaper he once owned and edited, died peacefully in hospital, aged 85 years.

His was a colourful career begun at the age of 11 years by selling newspapers in his Keighley, Yorkshire, home-town, and graduating which he was editor-proprietor of no fewer than 12 newspapers, in England, Scotland, and Wales.

He twice falsified his age in order to fight for his country in the two great wars. In the first he saw service in France and Ireland and was commissioned from the trenches.

In the second he was commissioned in the Royal Northumberland Fusiliers and saw service in France, Belgium, and Germany.

As a member of the army of occupation, he was put in charge of a large German circus, and organised performances for the troops and civilian population. On demobilisation, he moved to Tavistock, where he became editor-proprietor of the "Tavistock Times" and "East Cornwall Times" until 1962, when he sold the papers to a local newspaper group.

Tavistock Times and Gazette report the passing of Mr E. Whitaker (Uncle Jon) formerly proprietor and Editor of the Tavistock Times. (Courtesy Tavistock Library)

There are perils that can trap an inexperienced young reporter and I relate two instances, one where I was victim to misrepresentation and the other being subjected to threatening behaviour. A prominent 'Lady of the Manor' died in a village not far from Tavistock and her funeral was held at Tavistock Parish Church. In those days local reporters stood at the entrance and took the names of every person attending. Their names and often the wreath details as well would be published with a full report of the proceedings and a summary of the deceased's life. I shared this duty with the *Tavistock Gazette* reporter Mr 'Bill' Thraves who was fully experienced and very kindly gave me some useful tips on the numerous occasions we were in company. After the funeral the family invited us back to the manor and, not wanting to appear ungrateful and wishing to learn something to write about the lady who died, 'Bill' drove us out there. Family members were all over us, offering the choicest delicacies from the well laden table and informing us what a dearly beloved figure their late aunt or whatever had been. I duly wrote a heart-warming piece about her but was surprised to see Mr Thraves was more selective and brief in his report. Then the truth emerged when I was bombarded for days afterwards by irate parishioners from the same village, who told me what an 'old bat' she really was. I got the message and learned another lesson.

Another time there had been a road accident where a person was knocked down and badly injured. I knew who the driver was and unwisely named him in a preliminary report. The man concerned came to the office in a rage and went for me 'hammer and tongs', demanding to know where I got my information etc. It ended with him almost dragging me to the police station where he made a complaint. The officer we saw was Sergeant Thomas, a man big in stature, good hearted and highly respected by all who knew him. He looked me over in a fatherly way as he listened to my tormentor's ranting. 'Is what he says true?' was all he said before telling me I could go. I imagine he had a few words of advice to offer his informant and I heard no more about it. As for Mr Whitaker, he simply told me I should never disclose my sources of information and since then I have read of many instances where that principal was exercised by journalists whose identities were household names.

The most taxing of my duties were the several inquests I attended where I witnessed heart-breaking scenes when witnesses broke down and, in one instance, had to be literally carried away after giving evidence. They were the grandparents of a three-year-old boy who wandered away and drowned in their garden pond when their backs were turned only for an instant. I am now a grandparent myself and to this day I am against garden ponds where there might be toddlers present. In my very first two weeks in the job I attended four inquests on people I knew and respected. One was an elderly gentleman who lived in College Avenue, a very smart, quiet, courteous man. One afternoon he walked onto the Great Western railway line that ran across an embankment opposite the entrance to the Avenue, and calmly stood in front of a train and was killed. Another suicide was that of a well-known coal merchant who left a note for his wife while she was out shopping, to please call the police and direct them to a certain green on Tavistock golf course. They found his dead body there with a shotgun beside it.

Altogether my apprenticeship in journalism taught me much about human nature and life in general, with a lot of surprises along the way. But I was smitten by an overwhelming urge to travel and see foreign parts. Life in my home town and my job assignments were often invigorating but it wasn't enough for me and I craved adventure. Slowly my enthusiasm waned and my work suffered. Because my eyesight was not up to the required standard the Royal Marines and the Royal Navy would not accept me, but the Merchant Navy would take me as a catering rating. It was the only way I could realise my dream and I accordingly applied and was accepted at seventeen years of age. Mr Whitaker sat back and laughed when I told him saying 'I can see it Laddie – it's in your blood and good luck to you'. In retrospect it was the worst decision I ever made because I know he was anxious to groom me to take over the paper when he retired. Furthermore there would have been a far better future for me if I had stayed in journalism instead of roughing it at sea as a steward and being regarded as the lowest form of life on shipboard.

In the final weeks before going off to sea I worked at Pitts Cleave Quarry in the concrete department helping to make reinforced concrete posts. I spent a lot of time going to and fro' with a wheelbarrow, collecting concrete mix for the wooden moulds. It was hard work, but I was young and fit and besides, I needed the extra pay I was now getting to save up and pay for my uniform etc. when I went to the Sea Training School at Gravesend (there was no issue of uniform or working clothes in the Merchant Navy). All the men there were good solid workmen, cheerful and friendly. I was seconded to a particular area to work with a man called Ron Dawe, a wartime army veteran who pulled my leg a lot and taught me a lot as well. He smoked incessantly from a long cigarette holder and the fumes were heady and strong – I know because I tried it once (courtesy of Ron) and couldn't take it. It was EG ('Empire Grown') tobacco he smoked

Pitts Cleave Quarry. The offices (bottom right) are at the entrance from the Tavistock – Okehampton road and adjacent to the level crossing over the Tavistock – Launceston GWR railway line behind. (Courtesy of Mr R. Marks)

and the little shop he bought it from ordered it especially for him. I already knew several of the men there, including my old school friend Peter Howell's father who was an office employee; my future brother-in-law Ron Marks and his father worked together there; and good old 'Johnny' Waterfield (he with the fine tenor singing voice previously mentioned) was the level crossing gatekeeper and mess-room attendant. Most men took pies or pasties for their dinner at 12 o'clock and my own mother made me a meat and potato pie in a little dish every day; how she managed it I will never know but I suspect she went without to give it to me. Mr Waterfield collected each man's dish as he went in and when the whistle blew for dinner break they found their precious fare ready and piping hot. Some poor men had jam sandwiches.

I left Tavistock in November 1951 for the National Sea Training School at Gravesend in Kent with a light heart. I was going to see the world, but that is another story.

Acknowledgements

'The Yanks are Coming!'

Tavistock Museum.
Tavistock History Society.
Mr and Mrs E. Gafney, Abbotsfield Hall Nursing Home.
Dartmoor News, a bi-monthly local magazine.

History – Tavistock Market.

Tavistock Abbey by H. P. R. Finberg.
Tavistock and District History Society.
Devon County Library, Tavistock.
Mr Ian Maxted, Devon Local Studies Library, Exeter.
Devon Local Studies Web Site.
Mr D. Cross, Yelverton.
Mr Edwin Carruthers, Tavistock Market Reeve.
Messrs Ward and Chowen, Auctioneers, Tavistock.
Dartmoor News, a bi-monthly local magazine.

I also extend grateful thanks to the following:
My dearest wife June for her patience and understanding in all I have done.
My mother the late Mrs Kathleen James (*nee* Doidge).
Mr and Mrs R. Marks, Plymouth. My sister and brother-in-law.
Mr D. Harvey, Tavistock, and the late Mrs Glenda Harvey (*nee* Roberts) my cousin.
Mrs Cora McHugh (*nee* Doidge) my cousin.
Mr John Doidge, Newton Abbot (my cousin).
Mr R. Martin, Tavistock.
Mr K. Dickens, Tavistock.
Mr T. Hicks, Tavistock.
Mr G. Belshaw, Taunton.
Mr J. Powell, Tavistock, for information relating to *Western Morning News* production in Tavistock Pannier Market.
Mr George Rowland de Vey.
The National Railway Museum, York.
The Science and Social Picture Library, London.
The Fairground Heritage Centre, Lifton, Devon.

About the Author

Trevor James was born in Tavistock. He has had a varied career that included training as a Junior Reporter on the *Tavistock Times*, seven years in the Merchant Navy, six years factory work, twenty years in power stations (two of which were in Saudi Arabia), and ten years at Dartmoor Prison. He is married with three children and five grandchildren.

Now retired he has written six paperback books about Dartmoor Prison and numerous articles of local interest for *Dartmoor News*, a bi-monthly magazine circulated in the Dartmoor area. His other interests are English social history, local history, music, snooker, and until recently, walking on Dartmoor. This book was originally written for his grandchildren but on reflection he concluded that after more than sixty years, his experiences are part of a way of life gone forever and would have a wider appeal.

Also available from Amberley Publishing

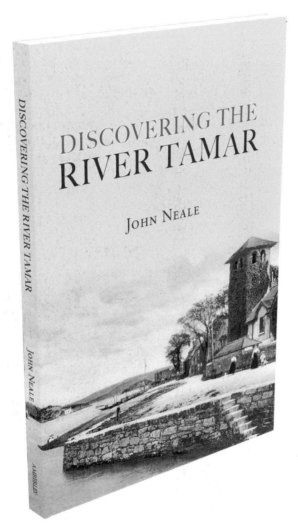

Available from all good bookshops, or order direct
from our website www.amberleybooks.com

Also available from Amberley Publishing

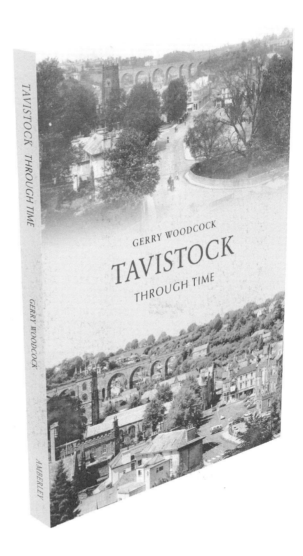

Also available from Amberley Publishing

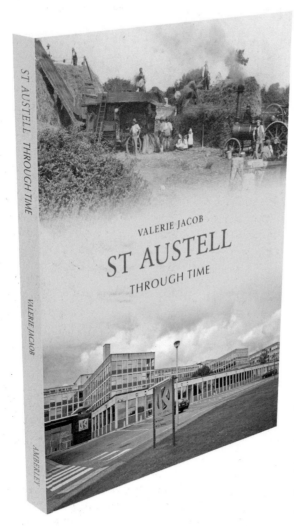

St Austell
Through Time
Valerie Jacob
ISBN: 978-1-84868-468-3
£12.99 PB